Reminiscences of Forts Sumter and Moultrie

FORT SUMTER

Reminiscences of Forts Sumter and Moultrie

The Opening Phase of the
American Civil War as experienced
by an officer of the Union Artillery

Abner Doubleday

LEONAUR

Reminiscences of
Forts Sumter
and Moultrie
The Opening Phase of the
American Civil War as experienced
by an officer of the Union Artillery
by Abner Doubleday

First published under the title
Reminiscences of
Forts Sumter
and Moultrie

Leonaur is an imprint
of Oakpast Ltd

ISBN: 978-1-84677-872-8 (hardcover)
ISBN: 978-1-84677-871-1 (softcover)

http://www.leonaur.com

Contents

Introduction

Now that the prejudices and bitter partisan feeling of the past are subsiding, it seems a fitting time to record the facts and incidents connected with the first conflict of the Rebellion. Of the eleven officers who took part in the events herein narrated, but four now survive. Before the hastening years shall have partially obliterated many circumstances from my memory, and while there is still an opportunity for conference and friendly criticism, I desire to make, from letters, memoranda, and documents in my possession, a statement which will embody my own recollections of the turbulent days of 1860 and 1861.

I am aware that later and more absorbing events have caused the earlier struggles of the war to recede in the distance; but those who were in active life at that time will not soon forget the thrill of emotion and sympathy which followed the movements of Anderson's little band, when it became its duty to unfold the flag of the Union against a united South in arms.

I know how difficult it is to write contemporaneous history, or even to give a bare detail of facts, without wounding the susceptibilities of others; but whenever I have felt called upon to give my own opinion, I have endeavoured to do so in the spirit of Lincoln's immortal sentiment—"With malice toward none; with charity for all."

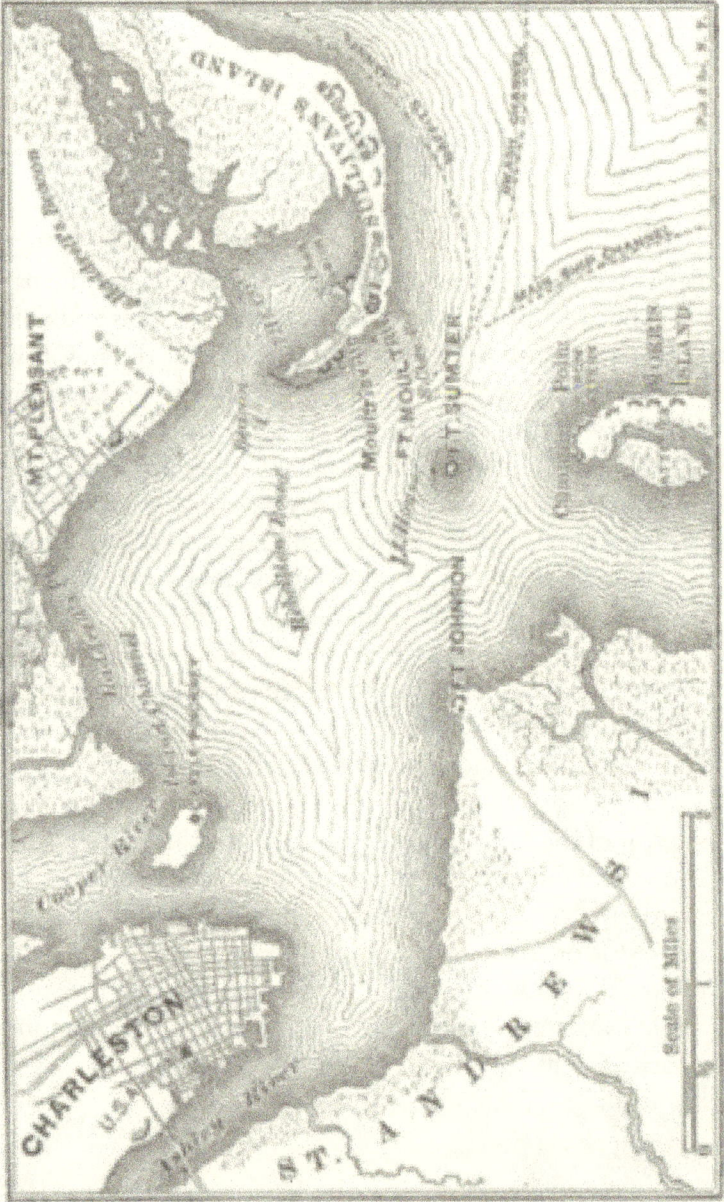

MAP OF CHARLESTON HARBOR

CHAPTER 1

Fort Moultrie in 1860

The summer of 1860 found me stationed at the head-quarters of the First United States Artillery at Fort Moultrie, South Carolina. I was captain of Company E, and second in command to Brevet Colonel John L. Gardner, who was lieutenant-colonel of the regiment. The regimental band and Captain Truman Seymour's company (H) also formed part of the garrison. The other forts were unoccupied, except by the ordnance-sergeants in charge.

Charleston, at this period, was far from being a pleasant place for a loyal man. Almost every public assemblage was tinctured with treasonable sentiments, and toasts against the flag were always warmly applauded. As early as July there was much talk of secession, accompanied with constant drilling, and threats of taking the forts as soon as a separation should occur.

To the South Carolinians Fort Moultrie was almost a sacred spot, endeared by many precious historical associations; for the ancestors of most of the principal families had fought there in the Revolutionary War behind their hastily improvised ramparts of palmetto logs, and had gained a glorious victory over the British fleet in its first attempt to enter the harbour and capture the city.

The modern fort had been built nearly on the site of the ancient one. Its walls were but twelve feet high. They were old, weak, and so full of cracks that it was quite common to see soldiers climb to the top by means of the support these crevices afforded to their hands and feet. The constant action of the sea-breeze had drifted one immense heap of sand against the shore-front of the work, and another in the immediate vicinity. These sand-hills dominated the parapet, and made the fort untenable. Indeed, it was originally built by the engineers as a mere sea-battery, with just sufficient strength to prevent it from being taken by a *coup de main*.

As an overpowering force of militia could always be summoned for its defence, it was supposed that no foreign army would ever attempt to besiege it. The contingency that the people of Charleston themselves might attack a fort intended for their own protection had never been anticipated.

Our force was pitifully small, even for a time of peace and for mere police purposes. It consisted of sixty-one enlisted men and seven officers, together with thirteen musicians of the regimental band; whereas the work called for a war garrison of three hundred men.

The first indication of actual danger came from Richmond, Virginia, in the shape of urgent inquiries as to the strength of our defences, and the number of available troops in the harbour. These questions were put by a resident of that city named Edmund Ruffin; an old man, whose later years had been devoted to the formation of disunion lodges, and who became subsequently noted for firing the first gun at Fort Sumter. His love of slavery amounted to fanaticism. When the cause of the Rebellion became hopeless, he refused to survive it, and committed suicide.

In the beginning of July, Robert Barnwell Rhett, and other ultra men in Charleston, made violent speeches to the mob, urging them to drive every United States official out of the State; but as many influential Secessionists were enjoying the sweets of Federal patronage under Buchanan, we did not anticipate any immediate disturbance. To influence his hearers still more, Rhett did not hesitate to state that Hamlin was a *mulatto*, and he asked if they intended to submit to a negro vice-president.[1]

It is an interesting question to know how far at this period

---

1. Hamlin's father named four of his sons, Europe, Asia, Africa, and America. The fact that one of them was called Africa gave rise to the statement that he was an African.

the Secretary of War himself was loyal. Mr. Dawson, the able editor of the *Historical Magazine*, is of opinion, after a careful investigation of the facts, that Floyd at this time was true to the Union, and that he remained so until December 24th, when it was discovered that he had been advancing large sums of money from the Treasury to contractors, to pay for work which had never been commenced. To make the loss good, nearly a million of dollars was taken from the Indian Trust Fund.

Finding he would be dismissed from the Cabinet for his complicity in these transactions, and would also be indicted by the Grand Jury of the District of Columbia, he made a furious Secession speech, sent in his resignation, and suddenly left for the South.[2] Mr. Dawson founds his opinion in this case upon the statement of Fitz John Porter, who was a major on duty in the War Department at the time, and therefore apparently well qualified to judge. Floyd's actions toward us, however, were not those of a true man, and I am of opinion that his loyalty was merely assumed for the occasion.

He sent seventeen thousand muskets to South Carolina, when he knew that Charleston was a hot-bed of sedition, and that in all probability the arms would be used against the United States. Greeley says, in his "American Conflict," that during these turbulent times Floyd disarmed the Government by forwarding one hundred and fifteen thousand muskets, in all, to the Southern Confederacy.[3] In addition to this, he sold large quantities of arms to S.B. Lamar, of Savannah, and other Secessionists in the South, on the plea that the muskets thus disposed of did not conform to the latest army model. Just before his resignation, he continued the same policy by directing that one hundred and twenty-four heavy guns should be shipped from Pittsburg,

---

2. He afterward returned, gave bail, and appeared before the court, because he was aware that a rule existed that parties who had given evidence before a Congressional committee in reference to any defalcation could not be tried for having taken part in it

3. It is true there is a law authorizing the distribution of *surplus* United States arms to the States, but there were no surplus muskets on hand; and even if there had been, it was a very injudicious time to distribute them among the insurgent States. A little delay would have been both patriotic and judicious..

Pennsylvania, to Ship Island, Mississippi, where there was no garrison, and to Galveston, Texas. Yet this was the official upon whom we were to rely for advice and protection. This was the wolf who was to guard the fold.

Our commander, Colonel Gardner, had done good service in the War of 1812 and in Mexico; but now, owing to his advanced age, was ill fitted to weather the storm that was about to burst upon us. In politics he was quite Southern, frequently asserting that the South had been treated outrageously in the question of the Territories, and defrauded of her just rights in other respects. He acquiesced, however, in the necessity of defending the fort should it be attacked; but as he lived with his family outside of the walls, he could not take a very active part himself. Indeed, on one occasion, when a Secession meeting was held in our immediate vicinity, accompanied with many threats and noisy demonstrations, he sent word to me to assume command at once in his place.

He now found himself in a peculiar position. The populace were becoming excited, and there was every probability that a collision, accidental or otherwise, might occur at any moment between the troops and the mob outside, if not between the troops and the State militia. The dilemma which confronted him was either to make a disgraceful surrender of his command, or take the other alternative, and fight South Carolina single-handed, without the aid or co-operation of the General Government. He thought the difficulty might perhaps be solved by removing the garrison to Smithville, North Carolina, having received permission to do so, in case the yellow fever, which had proved so disastrous the previous year, should break out again. Strange to say, some of the most ultra papers in the Southern interest in New York and Charleston ridiculed the proposed movement. They probably feared that our absence might deprive the conspirators of the prestige of an easy victory.

By the middle of August the country people began to be quite violent in their language, and made many threats of what they would do in case of Lincoln's election.

While the rebellion was thus drifting onward, the North remained quiescent, utterly refusing to believe in the existence of any real danger. Yet it was publicly known that, although the Southern States had refused to commit themselves to Secession, they were pledged not to allow South Carolina to be coerced, and this practically amounted to a powerful league against the Union, since it was a combination to prevent the enforcement of the laws which bound the States together.

As we were liable to be attacked at any moment, we desired to get rid of the sand-hills which dominated our walls. To this end we applied to the Quartermaster-general (General Joseph E. Johnston) for authority to hire citizen labourers; but he declined to accede to the request, on the ground that the work did not properly appertain to his department. He was a nephew of Floyd, and soon went over to the enemy. With the exception of Robert E. Lee, he subsequently became the most noted of all the rebel generals.

We were gratified, about the 1st of September, at seeing some signs of life in the Secretary of War, which seemed to show that he appreciated our dangers and difficulties. He ordered First Lieutenant and Brevet Captain John G. Foster, of the engineers, to repair to Fort Moultrie, and put that and the other defences of Charleston harbour in perfect order. The reason privately assigned for this was that we were drifting into complications with England and France with reference to Mexico. For one, I gave the honourable secretary very little credit for this proceeding, inasmuch as he had just previous to this forwarded to South Carolina the means of arming and equipping seventeen thousand men against the United States. I, therefore, came to the conclusion that the forts were to be made ready for active service, in order that they might be turned over in that condition to the Southern League.

Two young lieutenants of engineers, G.W. Snyder and R.K. Meade, were soon after sent to Foster as assistants.

And here it may be well to speak of the officers of our command, as they were at that period. The record of their services afterward, during the rebellion, would constitute a volume in itself.

Colonel John L. Gardner was wounded in the war with Great Britain in 1812. He had also been engaged in the war against the Florida Indians, and the war with Mexico, receiving two brevets for the battles of Cerro Gordo and Contreras.

Seymour, Foster, and myself had also served in Mexico as second lieutenants on our first entrance into the army, and Davis as a non-commissioned officer of an Indiana regiment.

John G. Foster, severely wounded at Molino del Rey, and brevetted captain, was one of the most fearless and reliable men in the service.

Captain Truman Seymour, twice brevetted for gallantry at Cerro Gordo and Chernbusco, was an excellent artillery officer, full of invention and resource, a lover of poetry, and an adept at music and painting.

First Lieutenant Jefferson C. Davis, brave, generous, and impetuous—the boy-sergeant of Buena Vista—won his first commission in the regular army by his gallantry in that action.

First Lieutenant Theodore Talbot, when very young, had shared the dangers, privations, and sufferings of Fremont's party in their explorations to open a pathway across the continent. He was a cultivated man, and a representative of the chivalry of Kentucky, equally ready to meet his friend at the festive board, or his enemy at ten paces.

Doctor S. Wiley Crawford, our assistant surgeon, entered the service after the Mexican war. He was a genial companion, studious, and full of varied information. His ambition to win a name as a soldier soon induced him to quit the ranks of the medical profession.

Hall, Snyder, and Meade were recent graduates of the Academy, who had never seen active service in the field. They were full of zeal, intelligence, and energy.

In one respect we were quite fortunate: the habits of the officers were good, and there was no dissipation or drunkenness in the garrison. The majority of the men, too, were old soldiers, who could be thoroughly relied upon under all circumstances.

There was, also, one civilian with us, Mr. Edward Moale, who was clerk and brother-in-law to Captain Foster. His services were subsequently very valuable in many ways.

Fearing that in the course of events our correspondence might be tampered with, I invented a cipher which afterward proved to be very useful. It enabled me to communicate, through my brother in New York, much valuable information to Mr. Lincoln at Springfield, Preston King, Roscoe Conkling, and other leaders of public opinion, in relation to our strength and resources.[4]

Situated as we were, we naturally desired to know how far Mr. Buchanan's Cabinet was willing to sustain us. William H. Trescott, of South Carolina, was Assistant Secretary of State at this time, and frequently corresponded with his brother, Doctor Trescott, in Charleston. We, therefore, naturally thought the views of the latter might indirectly reflect those of the Administration. The doctor was of opinion there would be no attempt at coercion in case South Carolina seceded, but that all postal and telegraphic communication would cease, and a man-of-war be placed outside to collect the revenue. This arrangement would leave our little force isolated and deserted, to bear the brunt of whatever might occur.

In October the disunionists became more bitter, but they were not disposed to be aggressive, as they thought Buchanan could be relied upon not to take any decisive action against them.

Colonel Gardner would not at this time mount the guns, or take any precautions whatever. He alleged, with reason, that the work was all torn to pieces by the engineers; that it was full of *débris*, and that, under the circumstances, he was not responsible for anything that might happen. We had been promised a considerable number of recruits, but they were kept back; and we now ascertained that none would be sent until late in December, after the crisis was over.

In the latter part of the month I became quite unpopular in Charleston; partly on account of my anti-slavery sentiments, but more especially because some very offensive articles, written

---

4. My brother and myself each owned copies of the same dictionary. Instead of using a word in my correspondence, I simply referred to its place in the book, by giving the number of the page, number of the column, and number of the word from the top of the page.

from that city, had appeared in the Northern papers, and were attributed to me. It seems that at this very time an abolition correspondent of the *New York Tribune* was employed in the office of Rhett's paper, the *Charleston Mercury*. This man professed to be the most loud-mouthed secessionist of them all. In conversation with me afterward, he claimed to be the author of the articles referred to.

In truth, these were days of extraordinary proscription for opinion's sake. I heard with profound indignation of the case of a poor seamstress from New York, who had been sent to jail in Charleston simply for stating that she did not believe in the institution of slavery. On appealing to the then mayor of New York, Fernando Wood, he replied that he was rejoiced she was in prison, and hoped she would be kept there.

Toward the close of the month, the South Carolina leaders began to fear that the other Southern States would not join them, and were engaged in discussing the subject of a French protectorate.

The negroes overheard a great deal that was said by their masters, and in consequence became excited and troublesome, for the news flew like wild-fire among them that "Massa Linkum" was coming to set them all free.

The enthusiasm of the moneyed men in Charleston began to cool when they reflected upon the enormous expenses involved in keeping up a standing army in an agricultural State like South Carolina. At the request of some Union men, Captain Seymour made a startling exhibit, showing the large amount required to maintain even a moderate force. It had a good effect upon the merchants, and, indeed, if the other Southern States had not promptly sustained South Carolina, the movement must have soon collapsed from its inherent weakness.

Although the secession leaders were preparing to meet coercion, if it should come, I will do them the justice to say that they determined to commit no overt act against the Union so long as the State formed an integral part of it. They soon found, however, that the mob did not recognize these fine distinctions. It was easy to raise the storm, but, once under full headway, it was difficult to govern it. Independent companies and minute-men were everywhere forming, in opposition to their wishes; for these organizations, from their very nature, were quite unmanageable.

The military commanders much preferred the State militia, because they could control it by law. A gentleman from the country, who had joined the minute-men, came in one day to the Charleston Hotel, with a huge cockade on his hat, expecting to be received with great applause; but, to his astonishment, he was greeted with laughter and ridicule.

On the 29th of October, General Scott wrote his celebrated letter to the President, recommending that strong garrisons be placed at once in all the Southern forts. Undoubtedly this was good advice; but as our army was widely scattered all over the West to protect the frontier settlements from the Indians, only five small companies were available for the purpose. The suggestion, therefore, had but little practical value.

November had arrived. The muttering of the storm was heard all around us, and yet not one word of counsel or encouragement came from Washington. Colonel Gardner began to feel uneasy at this studied silence, and determined to place the responsibility of any disaster that might occur where it properly belonged. On the 1st of the month he made a full report to his next superior officer, General Wool, at Troy, New York, to be forwarded to the Secretary of War, in relation to the dangers that threatened us, and our imperfect means of defence. He notified them that our provisions would be exhausted by the 20th of the month, and that we were very deficient in ammunition and military supplies generally.

The secretary, in his answer to this communication, simply expressed his regret that he had not been informed of all this before. This sympathy was no doubt very gratifying; but, being of an entirely passive nature, did not benefit us in the least. Colonel Gardner, at our solicitation, directed that the guns which had been dismounted to enable the engineers to make their repairs be remounted at once, and Seymour's company and mine soon placed them in position. It was of little use, however, to have our armament in readiness, unless the approaches to the fort could be carefully watched. This it was impossible to do by the ordinary system of guard duty; but I suggested a plan which enabled us to have an ample number of sentinels, without exhausting the men. It was done by placing each man on guard for a single hour, between tattoo and reveille, allowing him to sleep for the remainder of the night.

CHAPTER 2

Preparations for Defence

The United States Arsenal in Charleston is situated on the banks of the Ashley River. It looked feasible to go there in a boat without attracting attention, and procure a full supply of cartridges and other articles which were very much needed. Captain Seymour volunteered for the service, and was sent over with a small party, early in the afternoon. Notwithstanding he took every precaution, some spy belonging to a vigilance committee followed him, and reported the facts in the city. Seymour at once found himself beset by an excited mob, and wholly prevented from accomplishing the object of his mission.

Colonel Gardner wrote to Mayor Macbeth for an explanation. The latter apologized politely for this unexpected occurrence, and, speaking for himself and other city officials, stated that so long as they staid in the Union they desired to remain faithful to its obligations, and that no further obstacles would be thrown in the way of another expedition. Colonel Gardner, however, did not send out again, thinking, perhaps, the mob might be beyond the control of the mayor.

Since his arrival, Captain Foster had been hard at work on the fort. He had hired labourers from the vicinity of Charleston, and had sent to Baltimore for a large number of masons who had formerly worked for him. In spite of his efforts, we were still in a very weak condition, and unable to defend ourselves. It is true the sand had been removed from the sea-face of the work; but as that front had no flanking defences, the angles in the wall were torn down to enable the engineers to construct double *caponieres* there. This left great gaps, through which an assaulting party could penetrate at any moment. Perhaps in one sense it added to our security, for there was no glory to be acquired in capturing a fort which was wide open and defenceless. Crowds of excited countrymen, wearing secession cockades, constantly came to visit the work; and on the 3rd of November they formed in procession and marched around it, but did not offer any violence.

It may not be improper to state that I was the only officer of the command who favoured Lincoln's election. As regards my companions, however, there was no difference of opinion in regard to sustaining the new President should he be legally elected, and they were all both willing and anxious to defend the fort confided to their honour.

In view of the probable success of the Republican candidate for the presidency, Governor Gist called the South Carolina Legislature together, to meet on Monday, the 5th of November. In his message he recommended the immediate formation of a standing army of ten thousand men; and that all persons between the ages of eighteen and forty-five be armed for immediate service. In consequence of this recommendation, by the 9th of November the whole State was swarming with minutemen.

The spark came at last which was to set fire to the magazine. The startling news of Lincoln's election reached Charleston on the 7th of November. As this event was sure to lead to secession, the Disunionists were wild with delight. In their exuberance of spirits, they ran through the streets shouting "Hurra for Lincoln!" The United States District Court, which was in session, at once broke up, and its judge, Magrath, sent in his resignation. In the evening of the same day, Edmund Ruffin, who has already been referred to, made a fiery secession speech to an immense audience at the capitol of the State. The Legislature, inflamed by public sentiment, called a convention, to meet on the 17th of the month, to decide the question of secession. Governor Joseph E. Brown, of Georgia, also called a convention there for the same purpose; and the excitement in each State constantly reacted on the other.

In the early part of November, one hundred and fifty masons arrived from Baltimore to work on the forts in the harbour. They were undoubtedly good workmen, but it is much to be regretted that they were not also good Unionists. Captain Foster at this time did not believe that any serious complications would arise from the attitude South Carolina had assumed, and did not, therefore, think it necessary to pay any attention to the politics of his labourers. Had he selected zealous Union men, their arrival would have been a most opportune re-enforcement for the garrison. Unfortunately, most of them sympathized with the South, and their coming was rather a source of weakness than of strength, so far as actual fighting was concerned. They rendered us, however, great and timely assistance by their labour.

The first thing that attracted the eye of the stranger, upon approaching Charleston from the sea, was Fort Sumter. It was built on an artificial island made of large blocks of stone. The walls were of dark brick, and designed for three tiers of guns. The whole structure, as it rose abruptly out of the water, had a gloomy, prison-like appearance. It was situated on the edge of the channel, in the narrowest part of the harbour, between Fort Moultrie and Cummings Point, distant about a mile from the former place, and twelve hundred yards from the latter.

The year before, it had been used by us as a temporary place of confinement and security for some negroes that had been brought over from Africa in a slaver captured by one of our naval vessels. The inevitable conflict was very near breaking out at that time; for there was an eager desire on the part of all the people around us to seize these negroes, and distribute them among the plantations; and if the Government had not acted promptly in sending them back to Africa, I think an attempt would have been made to take them from us by force, on the ground that some of them had violated a State law by landing at Moultrieville.

As Fort Sumter has considerable historic renown, it may not be uninteresting to relate another incident connected with it, although it is not germane to my narrative. In 1859, after the

negroes were taken away, the fort remained in charge of an ordnance-sergeant, who lived there alone with his wife and two
little children. Supplies were sent to him regularly, but in case
of emergency he could only communicate with the shore by
means of a small boat. One wild stormy day, when the wind
was blowing a gale, he was suddenly struck down with yellow
fever. His wife saw that if he did not have immediate medical
assistance he would die. She herself could not go, as he required
constant attention, and the children were too young to be of
any service.

A day passed on, and it became evident that he was growing
worse. In a frantic state of mind, she rushed up to the top of the
fort, waved a sheet backward and forward, and raised and lowered the garrison flag repeatedly, in hopes of attracting the attention of some passing vessel; but although several went by, no
one seemed to notice the signals, or, if they did, they would not
stop, on account of the tempest, which still continued. She then
took the desperate resolution of putting her two little children
in the small boat, and trusting to the flood-tide to drift them
somewhere in the vicinity of Charleston. She placed a letter in
the hand of one of them, to be given to the first person they
met, imploring that a physician might be sent to her at once.
It was a terrible experiment, for the children might easily have
been swept out to sea by the ebb-tide before they could make
a landing. They succeeded, however, in reaching the shore near
Mount Pleasant. A doctor finally arrived, but too late to be of
any service.

Foster wanted forty muskets to arm some of his workmen, as
a guard for the powder in Fort Sumter, and for valuable public
property in Castle Pinckney. This was approved at Washington;
but the moment he obtained the guns from the arsenal, the
Secretary of War hastily telegraphed him, in the middle of the
night, to send them back again immediately. And yet at this same
period two thousand additional United States muskets were forwarded by Floyd's order to South Carolina; and the *Charleston
Courier* stated that five thousand more were on their way. This
did not look, much as if the Administration intended to sustain

us.

While the honourable secretary was thus supplying our enemies with arms, and leaving the United States Arsenal in Charleston, full of military stores, without a guard, he was very solicitous to ascertain whether our garrison duties were accurately performed, and sent an assistant inspector-general, Major Fitz John Porter, to make a thorough examination. As the secretary intended neither to re-enforce nor withdraw us, and as he made no effort at any time to remedy defects in our armament, this inspection seemed to us to be a mere pretence. It resulted, however, in relieving Colonel Gardner from his command, on Porter's recommendation, Major Robert Anderson being ordered to take his place.

Mr. Greeley was at this time the head of the Republican party, and one of the great leaders of Northern opinion. His immense services in rousing the public mind to the evils of slavery cannot be overestimated, but some of his views were too hastily formed and promulgated. In this crisis of our history he injured the cause he afterward so eloquently advocated by publishing an opinion, on the 9th of November, that the South had a perfect right to secede whenever a majority thought proper to do so; and, in another communication, he stated that the Union could not be pinned together with bayonets. General Scott was also at one time in favour of letting the "wayward sisters depart in peace;" and I have heard on good authority that at least one member of the Cabinet and one leading general, appalled by the magnitude of the conflict, were willing to consent to a separation, provided the Border States would go with the North. Greeley's article went farther than this, for it seemed to favour a simple severance of the North and the South.

This was not only a virtual abandonment of the rights of Northern men who had invested their capital in the Southern States, but it amounted to giving up all the sea-coast and magnificent harbours south of New Jersey, including Chesapeake Bay. It was expressing a willingness to surrender the mouth of the Mississippi, the commerce of the great North-west, and the Capitol at Washington, to the control of a foreign nation, hostile to us from the very nature of its institutions. In fact, it was a proposition to commit national suicide. The new Northern republic would have been three thousand miles long, and only one hundred miles wide, in the vicinity of Wheeling.

A country of such a peculiar shape could not, as every military man knows, have been successfully defended, and must inevitably have soon broken up into small confederacies. We objected, with reason, to the formation of a European monarchy in far-off Mexico, but the proposed separation would have created a powerful slave empire, with its northern border within eighteen miles of Philadelphia. Once firmly established there and along the Ohio, the Southern army could have burned Cincinnati from the opposite shore, and have penetrated to Lake Erie by a single successful battle and march, permanently severing the East from the West.

These unexpected views of Mr. Greeley strengthened the hands of the Disunionists. They were everywhere quoted as evidence that no attempt would be made to interfere with or coerce the South. The fearful and wavering were thus induced to join the clamorous majority.

I think, too, that the publication of these sentiments did much to influence the after-conduct of Major Anderson. He was not a Republican himself, and he may very well have thought, if the Republican leaders did not deny the right of secession, there was little use in his sacrificing his small command in a feeble attempt to make South Carolina remain in the Union.

The sky darkened after this, for Georgia voted a million of dollars to raise troops, and it became evident that the other Southern States would follow in the same direction.

By the 18th of November we considered ourselves reasonably secure against a *coup-de-main*. Our guns were up, and loaded with canister, and we had a fair supply of hand-grenades ready for use. With a view to intimidate those who were planning an attack, I occasionally fired toward the sea an eight-inch howitzer, loaded with double canister. The spattering of so many balls in the water looked very destructive, and startled and amazed the gaping crowds around. I also amused myself by making some

24

small mines, which would throw a shell a few feet out of the ground whenever any person accidentally trod upon a concealed plank: of course the shell did not have a bursting charge in it. These experiments had a cooling effect upon the ardour of the militia, who did not fancy storming the fort over a line of torpedoes.

CHAPTER 3

Preliminary Movements of the Secessionists

It was now openly proclaimed in Charleston that declarations in favour of the Union would no longer be tolerated; that the time for deliberation had passed, and the time for action had come.

On the 21st our new commander arrived and assumed command. He felt as if he had a hereditary right to be there, for his father had distinguished himself in the Revolutionary War in defence of old Fort Moultrie against the British, and had been confined a long time as a prisoner in Charleston. We had long known Anderson as a gentleman; courteous, honest, intelligent, and thoroughly versed in his profession. He had been twice brevetted for gallantry—once for services against the Seminole Indians in Florida, and once for the battle of Molino del Rey in Mexico, where he was badly wounded.

In politics he was a strong pro-slavery man. Nevertheless, he was opposed to secession and Southern extremists. He soon found himself in troubled waters, for the approaching battle of Fort Moultrie was talked of everywhere throughout the State, and the mob in Charleston could hardly be restrained from making an immediate assault. They were kept back once through the exertions of Colonel Benjamin Huger, of the Ordnance Department of the United States Army. As he belonged to one of the most distinguished families in Charleston, he had great influence there.

It was said at the time that he threatened if we were attacked, or rather mobbed, in this way, he would join us, and fight by the side of his friend Anderson.[1] Colonel Memminger, afterward the Confederate Secretary of the Treasury, also exerted himself to prevent any irregular and unauthorized violence.

An additional force of workmen having arrived from Baltimore, Captain Foster retained one hundred and twenty to continue the work on Fort Moultrie, leaving his assistant, Lieutenant Snyder, one hundred and nine men to finish Fort Sumter.

On the 1st of December, Major Anderson made a full report to Secretary Floyd in relation to our condition and resources. It was accompanied with requisitions, in due form, for supplies and military material. Colonel Gardner, before he left, had already applied for rations for the entire command for six months.

Previous to Lincoln's election, Governor Gist had stated that in that event the State would undoubtedly secede, and demand the forts, and that any hesitation or delay in giving them up would lead to an immediate assault. Active preparations were now in progress to carry out this threat. In the first week of December we learned that cannon had been secretly sent to the northern extremity of the island, to guard the channel and oppose the passage of any vessels bringing us re-enforcements by that entrance. We learned, too, that lines of countervallation had been quietly marked out at night, with a view to attack the fort by regular approaches in case the first assault failed.

Also, that two thousand of the best riflemen in the State were engaged to occupy an adjacent sand-hill and the roofs of the adjoining houses, all of which overlooked the parapet, the intention being to shoot us down the moment we attempted to man our guns. Yet the Administration made no arrangements to withdraw us, and no effort to re-enforce us, because to do the former would excite great indignation in the North, and the latter might be treated as coercion by the South. So we were

---

1. He left the United States service soon after the attack on Fort Sumter, and joined the Confederates. He did so reluctantly, for he had gained great renown in our army for his gallantry in Mexico, and he knew he would soon have been promoted to the position of Chief of our Ordnance Department had he remained with us.

left to our own scanty resources, with every probability that the affair would end in a massacre. Under these circumstances the appropriating of $150,000 to repair Fort Moultrie and $80,000 to finish Fort Sumter by the mere order of the Secretary of War, without the authority of Congress, was simply an expenditure of public money for the benefit of the Secessionists, and I have no doubt it was so intended. Forts constructed in an enemy's country, and left unguarded, are built for the enemy.

Congress met on the 3rd of December, but took no action in relation to our peculiar position. As usual, their whole idea was to settle the matter by some new compromise. The old experiment was to be tried over again: St. Michael and the Dragon were to lie down in peace, and become boon companions once more.

The office-holders in the South, who saw in Lincoln's election an end to their pay and emoluments, were Secessionists to a man, and did their best to keep up the excitement. They tried to make the poor whites believe that through the re-opening of the African slave-trade negroes would be for sale, in a short time, at thirty dollars a head; and that every labouring man would soon become a rich slave-owner and cotton-planter. To the timid, they said there would be no coercion. To the ambitious, they spoke of military glory, and the formation of a vast slave empire, to include Mexico, Central America, and the West Indies. The merchants were assured that Charleston would be a free port, rivalling New York in its trade and opulence.

They painted the future in glowing colours, but the present looked dreary enough. All business was at an end. The expenses of the State had become enormous, and financial ruin was rapidly approaching. The heavy property-owners began to fear they might have to bear the brunt of all these military preparations in the way of forced loans.[2] For a time a strong reaction set in against the Rhett faction, but intimidation and threats prevented any open retrograde movement.

---

2. About a month afterward the Honourable William Aiken, who was a Union man, and who had formerly been governor of the State, and a member of Congress, was compelled to pay forty thousand dollars as his share of the war taxes.

Among those who were reported to be most clamorous to have an immediate attack made upon us, was a certain captain of the United States Dragoons, named Lucius B. Northrup; afterward made Paymaster-general of South Carolina, and subsequently, through the personal friendship of Jeff. Davis, promoted to be Commissary-general of the rebel army. He had resided for several years in Charleston on sick-leave, on full pay. Before urging an assault he should have had the grace to resign his commission, for his oath of office bound him to be a friend to his comrades in the army, and not an enemy.

I am tempted, in this connection, to show how differently the rebel general Magruder acted, under similar circumstances, when he was a captain and brevet colonel in our service. He said to his officers, the evening before he rode over the Long Bridge, at Washington, to join the Confederates, "If the rebels come tonight, we'll give them hell; but tomorrow I shall send in my resignation, and become a rebel myself."

Amidst all this turmoil, our little band of regulars kept their spirits up, and determined to fight it out to the last against any force that might be brought against them. The brick-layers, however, at work in Fort Sumter were considerably frightened. They held a meeting, and resolved to defend themselves, if attacked by the Charleston roughs, but not to resist any organized force.

On the 11th of December we had the good fortune to get our provisions from town without exciting observation. They had been lying there several days. It was afterward stated in the papers that the captain of the schooner was threatened severely for having brought them. On the same day the enemy began to build batteries at Mount Pleasant, and at the upper end of Sullivan's Island, guns having already been sent there. We also heard that ladders had been provided for parties to escalade our walls. Indeed, the proposed attack was no longer a secret. Gentlemen from the city said to us, "We appreciate your position. It is a point of honour with you to hold the fort, but a political necessity obliges us to take it."

My wife, becoming indignant at these preparations, and the utter apathy of the Government in regard to our affairs, wrote a stirring letter to my brother, in New York, stating some of the facts I have mentioned. By some means it found its way into the columns of the *Evening Post*, and did much to call attention to the subject, and awaken the Northern people to a true sense of the situation. She was quite distressed to find her hasty expressions in print, and freely commented on both by friends and enemies. I may say, in passing, that the distinguished editor of that paper, William Cullen Bryant, proved to be one of the best friends we had at the North. George W. Curtis, who aided us freely with his pen and influence, was another. They exerted themselves to benefit us in every way, and were among the first to invoke the patriotism of the nation to extricate us from our difficulties, and save the union of the States. When we returned to New York, they and their friends gave us a cordial and heartfelt welcome.

To resume the thread of my narrative. The fort by this time had been considerably strengthened. The crevices were filled up, and the walls were made sixteen feet high, by digging down to the foundations and throwing up the surplus earth as a glacis. Each of the officers had a certain portion given him to defend. I caused a sloping picket fence, technically called *a fraise*, to be projected over the parapet on my side of the work, as an obstacle against an escalading party. I understood that this puzzled the military men and newspapers in Charleston exceedingly. They could not imagine what object I could have in view. One of the editors said, in reference to it, "Make ready your sharpened stakes, but you will not intimidate freemen."

There was one good reason why our opponents did not desire to commence immediate hostilities. The delay was manifestly to their advantage, for the engineers were putting Fort Sumter in good condition at the expense of the United States. They (the rebels) intended to occupy it as soon as the work approached completion. In the mean time, to prevent our anticipating them, they kept two steamers on guard, to patrol the harbour, and keep us from crossing. These boats contained one hundred and twenty soldiers, and were under the command of Ex-lieutenant James Hamilton, who had recently resigned from the United States Navy.

The threatening movements against Fort Moultrie required incessant vigilance on our part, and we were frequently worn out with watching and fatigue. On one of these occasions Mrs. Seymour and Mrs. Doubleday volunteered to take the places of Captain Seymour and myself, and they took turns in walking the parapet, two hours at a time, in readiness to notify the guard in case the minute-men became more than usually demonstrative.

In December the secretary sent another officer of the Inspector-general's Department, Major Don Carlos Buell, to examine and report upon our condition. Buell bore written orders, which were presented on the 11th, directing Major Anderson not to provoke hostilities, but in case of immediate danger to defend himself to the last extremity, and take any steps that he might think necessary for that purpose. There would appear to be some mystery connected with this subject, for Anderson afterward stated to Seymour, as a reason for not firing when the rebels attempted to sink the *Star of the West*, that his instructions tied his hands, and obliged him to remain quiescent.

Now, as there are no orders of this character on record in the War Department, they must have been of a verbal and confidential nature. In my opinion, Floyd was fully capable of supplementing written orders to resist, by verbal orders to surrender without resistance. If he did so, I can conceive of nothing more treacherous, for his object must have been to make Anderson the scapegoat of whatever might occur. Buell, however, is not the man to be the bearer of any treacherous communication. Still, he did not appear to sympathize much with us, for he expressed his disapproval of our defensive preparations; referring particularly to some loop-holes near the guard-house, which he said would have a tendency to irritate the people. I thought the remark a strange one, under the circumstances, as "the people" were preparing to attack us. I had no doubt, at the time, in spite of the warlike message he had brought, that Buell's expressions reflected the wishes of his superiors.

I have ascertained recently that Floyd did have one or more

confidential agents in Charleston, who were secretly intermeddling in this matter, without the sanction of the President or the open authority of the War Office. It appears from the records that another assistant adjutant-general, Captain Withers, who joined the rebels at the outbreak of the rebellion, and became a rebel general, was also sent by Floyd to confer with Anderson. It is not at all improbable, therefore, that some one of the messengers who actually joined the enemy may have been the bearer of a treasonable communication.

It appears from Anderson's own statement that his hands were tied, and no one that knew him would ever doubt his veracity. Yet, if he really desired to retain possession of Charleston Harbor for the Government, and Floyd's orders stood in his way, why did he not, after the latter fled to the South, make a plain statement to the new secretary, Judge Holt, whose patriotism was undoubted, and ask for fresh instructions? It looks to me very much as if he accepted the orders without question because he preferred the policy of non-resistance.

I shall have occasion to refer to this subject again in the course of my narrative.

We had frequently regretted the absence of a garrison in Castle Pinckney, as that post, being within a mile of Charleston, could easily control the city by means of its mortars and heavy guns. We were too short-handed ourselves to spare a single soldier. The brave ordnance-sergeant, Skillen, who was in charge there, begged hard that we would send him a few artillerists. He could not bear the thought of surrendering the work to the enemies of the Government without a struggle, and would have made a determined resistance if he could have found any one to stand by him. We talked the matter over, and Captain Foster thought he could re-enforce Skillen by selecting a few reliable men from his masons to assist in defending the place.

He accordingly sent a body of picked workmen there, under his assistant, Lieutenant R.K. Meade, with orders to make certain repairs. The moment, however, Meade attempted to teach these men the drill at the heavy guns, they drew back in great alarm, and it was soon seen that no dependence could be placed upon them. So Castle Pinckney was left to its fate.

As the General Government seemed quietly to have deserted us, we watched the public sentiment at the North with much interest. There was but little to encourage us there. The Northern cities, however, were beginning to appreciate the gravity of the crisis. At the call of the Mayor of Philadelphia, a great public meeting was held in Independence Square. For one, I was thoroughly dispirited and disgusted at the resolutions that were passed. They were evidently prompted by the almighty dollar, and the fear of losing the Southern trade. They urged that the North should be more than ever subservient to the South, more active in catching fugitive slaves, and more careful not to speak against the institution of slavery. As a pendant to these resolutions, an official attempt was made, a few days afterward, to prevent the eloquent Republican orator, George W. Curtis, from advocating the Northern side of the question.

Chapter 4

The Removal to Fort Sumter

On the 17th a bill was passed to arm the militia of North Carolina.

On the same day the Charleston Convention met, and chose General D.F. Jamison as their president, and on the 20th of the month the secession ordinance was duly passed, and South Carolina voted out of the Union amidst screams of enthusiasm. Immediately afterward there was great competition for the possession of the immortal pen with which the instrument was signed. At the close of the war, I heard it was for sale at a very low figure.

The new Governor, Francis W. Pickens, signed the ordinance very gladly, and issued his proclamation on the 24th declaring South Carolina to be a free and independent nation. He had served as a member of Congress from 1835 to 1843, and as Minister to Russia in 1858, but he was not considered a man of decided ability. He was very impetuous in his disposition, and, according to a statement made by him in one of his Congressional speeches, which attracted much attention at the time, he was "born insensible to fear."

Soon after the State seceded, that stern old patriot, Judge J.L. Petigru, of South Carolina, came over, with one of his friends, to pay us a final visit, to express the deep sorrow and sympathy he felt for us in our trying position. As he knew that arrangements were being made to drive us out, he bade us farewell with much feeling. The tears rolled down his cheeks as he deplored the folly and the madness of the times. He had been previously asked in the city if he did not intend to join the secession movement. He replied, "*I should think not! South Carolina is too small for a republic, and too large for a lunatic-asylum.*"

At a later period of the war, it is said he was called upon to give up the property of his Northern clients for confiscation, under a law which made it treason to refuse. He positively declined to comply with the demand, and said, with much spirit, "*Whenever the time comes for me to choose between death and dishonour, I shall have no difficulty in saying which of the two I shall elect.*" It is much to be regretted that he did not live to witness the final triumph of the cause which was so dear to him.

Four of Buchanan's Cabinet—Floyd, Cobb, Toucey, and Thompson—were now open and avowed Disunionists. On the 23rd, a defalcation of eight hundred and thirty-three thousand dollars was discovered in the Department of the Interior, while the Secretary, Jacob Thompson, was absent from his post, and acting as a disunion agent, to represent the State of Mississippi. This dallying with treason in the Cabinet was one of the most discouraging signs of the times.

A circumstance now occurred which to my mind was proof positive that Floyd intended to betray us and the Government he represented. I have no doubt it hastened our departure from Fort Moultrie. He directed Captain Foster to have the guns mounted in Fort Sumter immediately. It was plain enough, from demonstrations already made, that the moment this was done the rebels would seize the fort, and turn its powerful armament upon us. There was no one there to resist them. It seems to me that Floyd's speech to the Secessionists of Richmond, made shortly after his flight from Washington, was a pretty plain acknowledgment that he had violated his oath of office as Secretary of War, in order that he might advance the interests of the Confederacy. He said on that occasion, "I undertook so to dispose of the power in my hands that when the terrific hour came, you, and all of you, and each of you, should say, 'This man has done his duty.'"

Anderson had been urged by several of us to remove his command to Fort Sumter, but he had invariably replied that he was specially assigned to Fort Moultrie, and had no right to vacate it without orders. Our affairs, however, were becoming critical, and I thought it my duty to speak to him again on the subject. He still apparently adhered to his decision. Nevertheless, he had fully determined to make the change, and was now merely awaiting a favourable opportunity. To deceive the enemy, he still kept at work with unabated zeal on the defences of Fort Moultrie. This exactly suited the purposes of the rebel leaders, for they knew we could make no effectual defence there, and our preparations would only increase the prestige of their victory.

We were not authorized to commence hostilities by burning the adjacent houses, and yet, if they were not levelled, clouds of riflemen could occupy them, and prevent our men from serving the guns. Under any circumstances, it was plain that we must soon succumb from over-exertion and loss of sleep incident to repelling incessant attacks from a host of enemies. The fact that through the provident care of the Secretary of War the guns of Fort Sumter would also be turned upon us, enfilading two sides of Fort Moultrie, and taking another side in reverse, was quite decisive as to the impossibility of our making a lengthened defence.

Up to this time we had hoped, almost against hope, that, even if the Government were base enough to desert us, the loyal spirit of the patriotic North would manifest itself in our favour, inasmuch as our little force represented the supremacy of the Constitution and the laws; but all seemed doubt, apathy, and confusion there. Yancey was delivering lectures in the Northern States, as a representative of the Disunionists, not only without molestation, but with frequent and vociferous applause from the Democratic masses, who could not be made to believe there was any real danger.

In making his arrangements to cross over, Anderson acted with consummate prudence and ability. He only communicated his design to the staff-officers, whose co-operation was indispensable, and he waited until the moment of execution before he informed the others of his intention. No one, of course, would deliberately betray a secret of this kind, but it sometimes happens, under such circumstances, that officers give indications of what is about to take place by sending for their washing, packing their trunks, and making changes in their messing arrangements.

Without knowing positively that any movement had been projected, two circumstances excited my suspicions. Once, while I was walking with the major on the parapet, he turned to me abruptly, and asked me what would be the best course to take to render the gun-carriages unserviceable. I told him there were several methods, but my plan would be to heap pitch-pine knots around them, and burn them up. The question was too suggestive to escape my attention.

On the day previous to our departure, I requested him to allow me to purchase a large quantity of wire, to make an entanglement in front of the part of the work I was assigned to defend. He said, with a quizzical look, "Certainly; you shall have a mile of wire, if you require it." When I proposed to send for it immediately, he smiled, and objected in such a peculiar way that I at once saw that he was no longer interested in our efforts to strengthen Fort Moultrie.

As a preliminary to the proposed movement, he directed the post quartermaster, Lieutenant Hall, to charter three schooners and some barges, for the ostensible purpose of transporting the soldiers' families to old Fort Johnson, on the opposite side of the harbour, where there were some dilapidated public buildings belonging to the United States. The danger of the approaching conflict was a good pretext for the removal of the non-combatants. All this seemed natural enough to the enemy, and no one offered any opposition. In reality, these vessels were loaded with supplies for all the troops, with reference to a prolonged residence in Fort Sumter. Hall was directed to land everything there as soon as a signal-gun was fired. In the mean time he sailed for Fort Johnson, and lay off and on, waiting for the signal.

Anderson had broken up his own mess, and on the last evening of our stay (December 26th) I left my room to ask him in to take tea with us. The sun was just setting as I ascended the steps leading to the parapet and approached him. He was in the midst of a group of officers, each of whom seemed silent and distrait. As I passed our assistant-surgeon, I remarked, "It is a fine evening, Crawford." He replied in a hesitating and embarrassed manner, showing that his thoughts were elsewhere. I saw plainly that something unusual had occurred. Anderson approached me as I advanced, and said quietly, "I have determined to evacuate this post immediately, for the purpose of occupying Fort Sumter; I can only allow you twenty minutes to form your company and be in readiness to start."

I was surprised at this announcement, and realized the gravity of the situation at a glance. We were watched by spies and vigilance-committees, who would undoubtedly open fire upon us as soon as they saw the object of the movement. I was naturally concerned, too, for the safety of my wife, who was the only lady in the fort at that time, and who would necessarily be exposed to considerable danger. Fortunately, I had little or no property to lose, as, in anticipation of a crisis, I had previously sent everything of value to New York. Some of the other officers did not fare so well. The doctor, not expecting so sudden a *dénouement*, had necessarily left his medical stores unpacked. Foster, who had taken a house outside for his family, was wholly unprepared, and lost heavily.

I made good use of the twenty minutes allowed me. I first went to the barracks, formed my company, inspected it, and saw that each man was properly armed and equipped. This left me ten minutes to spare. I dashed over to my quarters; told my wife to get ready to leave immediately, and as the fighting would probably commence in a few minutes, I advised her to take refuge with some family outside, and get behind the sand-hills as soon as possible, to avoid the shot. She hastily threw her wearing-apparel into her trunks, and I called two men to put her baggage outside the main gate. I then accompanied her there, and we took a sad and hasty leave of each other, for neither knew when or where we would meet again. As soon as this was accomplished, I strapped on my revolver, tied a blanket across my shoulders, and reported to Major Anderson that my men were in readiness to move.

In the meantime Lieutenant Jefferson C. Davis, of my company, who had been detailed to command the rear guard, aimed the guns, which were already loaded, to bear upon the passage to Fort Sumter, and Captain Foster and Assistant-surgeon Crawford, with two sergeants and three privates, remained with him, and took post at five *columbiads*, in readiness to carry out Major Anderson's design, which was to sink the guard-boats, should they attempt to fire into us or run us down while *en route*. Certainly the major showed no lack of determination or energy on this occasion.

If we were successful in crossing, Davis was to follow with the remainder of the men. Foster and Mr. Moale agreed to remain behind until morning. They also volunteered to place themselves at the guns, and cover the retreat of the rear guard under Davis, in case an attempt was made to intercept them.

The chaplain, the Rev. Matthias Harris, being a non-combatant, and having his family in the village, was not notified. Neither was Surgeon Simons, of the army, who was living in a house adjoining the fort, and directly in line with our guns. When he saw the movement in progress, he hastened out with his family, to shelter them behind the sand-hills as soon as possible.

Everything being in readiness, we passed out of the main gates, and silently made our way for about a quarter of a mile to a spot where the boats were hidden behind an irregular pile of rocks, which originally formed part of the sea-wall. There was not a single human being in sight as we marched to the rendezvous, and we had the extraordinary good luck to be wholly unobserved. We found several boats awaiting us, under charge of two engineer officers, Lieutenants Snyder and Meade. They and their crews were crouched down behind the rocks, to escape observation. In a low tone they pointed out to me the boats intended for my company, and then pushed out rapidly to return to the fort.

Noticing that one of the guard-boats was approaching, they made a wide circuit to avoid it. I hoped there would be time for my party to cross before the steamer could overhaul us; but as among my men there were a number of unskilful oarsmen, we made but slow progress, and it soon became evident that we would be overtaken in mid-channel. It was after sunset, and the twilight had deepened, so that there was a fair chance for us to escape. While the steamer was yet afar off, I took off my cap, and threw open my coat to conceal the buttons. I also made the men take off their coats, and use them to cover up their muskets, which were lying alongside the rowlocks. I hoped in this way that we might pass for a party of labourers returning to the fort.

The paddle-wheels stopped within about a hundred yards of us; but, to our great relief, after a slight scrutiny, the steamer kept on its way. In the mean time our men redoubled their efforts, and we soon arrived at our destination. As we ascended the steps of the wharf, crowds of workmen rushed out to meet us, most of them wearing secession emblems.

One or two Union men among them cheered lustily, but the majority called out angrily, "What are these soldiers doing here?" I at once formed my men, charged bayonets, drove the tumultuous mass inside the fort, and seized the guard-room, which commanded the main entrance. I then placed sentinels to prevent the crowd from encroaching on us. As soon as we had disembarked, the boats were sent back for Seymour's company. The major landed soon after in one of the engineer boats, which had coasted along to avoid the steamer. Seymour's men arrived in safety, followed soon after by the remaining detachments, which had been left behind as a rear-guard. The latter, however, ran a good deal of risk, for in the dark it passed almost under the bow of the guard-boat *Niña*.

The whole movement was successful beyond our most sanguine expectations, and we were highly elated. The signal-gun was fired, and Hall at once sailed over, and landed the soldiers' families and supplies. As soon as the schooners were unloaded, the disloyal workmen were placed on board and shipped off to the mainland. Only a few of the best and most reliable were retained.

Upon leaving me, my wife took refuge temporarily in the

residence of Dan Sinclair, the sutler of the post, a most excellent man, and one to whom we were indebted for many kindnesses. Finding that the people of Moultrieville were not yet aware of the change that had taken place, and that everything was tranquil, she ventured back to the fort, and finished the removal of all our effects. After this, in company with the chaplain's family, she walked up and down the beach the greater part of the night, looking anxiously toward Fort Sumter to see if there were any indications of trouble or disturbance there. In the morning she took up her residence at the chaplain's house. As for the other ladies, both Mrs. Simons and Mrs. Foster fled to the city at the first intimation of danger, and Mrs. Seymour was already there.

CHAPTER 5

The First Overt Act

On the very day that these events occurred, the South Carolina commissioners, R.W. Barnwell, J.H. Adams, and James L. Orr, arrived in Washington to treat for the surrender of the forts and other public property. It proved to be a very inauspicious time for such a negotiation.

Our garrison were up betimes on the morning of the 27th, to inspect their new quarters. The soldiers thronged the parapet in such numbers as to attract the attention of the troops on board the *Niña*. That vessel steamed up to the city in great haste, and communicated the startling intelligence that Fort Sumter, in some inexplicable manner, had been fully re-enforced.[1] The chagrin of the authorities was intense. Messengers were at once dispatched to all parts of the city, to ring the door-bells and arouse the people.

While this was going on in town, Anderson, who was very punctilious in regard to settling all debts due by the United States to citizens, determined to send a detachment, under Lieutenant Davis, back to Fort Moultrie as a guard to Captain Foster, to enable him to pay off the claims of the workmen he had left behind. Doctor Crawford went over also, to look after some of his medical property. As the guard-boats had been withdrawn, they reached the fort without difficulty, and found it deserted.

The people of the little village, to all appearance, were still ignorant of our change of station. Soon after their arrival, the par-

---

1. Dawson's *Historical Magazine.*

ty, in accordance with instructions from Major Anderson, set fire to the gun-carriages bearing on Fort Sumter, and destroyed all the ammunition and military material that could not be brought away. The guns had been spiked the night before, and the flag-staff was cut down, either at that time or in the morning.

As I have stated, the major took great pains to see that all bills, even those of a private nature, due in Charleston we're fully paid by the officers and men of his command; but many leading merchants in the city were not so scrupulous. They gladly took advantage of the war to repudiate the claims of their Northern creditors. I was also informed by one of the pay-masters that a number of officers of the army who resigned to join the rebellion first deliberately drew their month's pay in advance, and then left the pay-master, as a penalty for his kindness, to make good the deficiency from his private funds, in order to settle his accounts.

Foster and Davis, finding Fort Moultrie still deserted, made good use of the occasion by loading up with supplies and ammunition one of the schooners which had been previously chartered to carry over the women and children, and which were now lying empty at the wharf.

On their way back from this expedition our officers saw the Charleston troops going over to take possession of Castle Pinckney. The calm and dignified South Carolina Legislature had not authorized this outrageous proceeding. Even if we assume that the State had the right to secede, it does not follow that the public property within her limits properly belonged to her. It appertained to the nation at large, inasmuch as all the other States had contributed toward it, and therefore it was a proper subject of negotiation. To seize it at once, without a declaration of war, and while the subject was still pending, was a violation of all right and precedent.

The hot-headed governor, however, irritated at our change of station, took the responsibility of commencing hostilities against the Union, without the co-operation of the Legislature, and this, too, at a time when the State was almost destitute of war material and funds. I doubt if there were more than half a dozen heavy guns on hand, and there were certainly not a dozen rounds of cannon-powder for each.

Major Anderson, who was a very religious man, thought it best to give some solemnity to our occupation of Fort Sumter by formally raising the flag, at noon, with prayer and military ceremonies. The band played "The Star-spangled Banner," the troops presented arms, and our chaplain, the Rev. Matthias Harris, offered up a fervent supplication, invoking the blessing of Heaven upon our small command and the cause we represented. Three cheers were then given for the flag, and the troops were dismissed.

The seizure of Castle Pinckney, on the afternoon of the 27th, was the first overt act of the Secessionists against the sovereignty of the United States. As already stated, it was ordered by Governor Pickens, on his own responsibility, without the concurrence of the Legislature.[2] The latter, indeed, positively declined to sanction the measure. At 2 p.m. the Washington Light Infantry and Meagher Guards, both companies of Colonel J.J. Petigru's rifle regiment, embarked, under command of that officer, on board the *Niña*, and steamed down to the little island upon which the castle is situated.

When they arrived in front of the main gates they found them closed; whereupon they applied scaling-ladders, and with eager, flushed faces made their way to the top of the wall. The excitement was needless, for there was no one there to resist them, the only fighting-men present being Lieutenant R.K. Meade, of the engineers, and Ordnance-sergeant Skillen, who resided there with his family, and who was in charge of the work. Meade, himself a Virginian, had a sharp colloquy with Petigru, and expressed himself in severe terms in relation to this treasonable assault.

After taking possession, one of the rebel officers found the sergeant's daughter, pretty Kate Skillen, aged fifteen, weeping bitterly at the foot of the ramparts. He assured her no harm should befall her. She replied, "I am not crying because I am afraid!"

2. See Dawson's story of Fort Sumter, in the *Historical Magazine for January, 1872.*

"What is the matter, then?" said he.

"I am crying because you have put that miserable rag up there," she said, pointing to the Palmetto flag which had just been raised to the top of the staff.

Foster's few reliable workmen proved to be a bad investment. It is said that most of them, when they found the enemy were actually coming, hid in closets, sheds, and under the beds, and some cried bitterly.

While this was going on, Major Anderson and myself stood side by side on the parapet, watching the scene through our spy-glasses. From his expressions of indignation, I was in hopes he would take prompt measures to close the harbour against any further encroachments of the State troops, made with a view to occupy Fort Moultrie or Fort Johnson. It would have required but a short time to mount a few pieces; and when these were once in position, it would have been easy to cut off all direct communication by water between the different posts. In short, he could take entire possession of the harbour. He did threaten to put out the lights in the light-houses with his artillery, and close the port in that way; but his anger soon passed away, and he took no aggressive measures of any kind.

In my opinion, if he could have been satisfied that no other States would join South Carolina in her mad attempt, he would have done everything that lay in his power to punish her; for he looked upon her as a spoiled child that needed correction. Having married a lady from Georgia, he had almost identified himself with that State. He did own a plantation and negroes there, but had recently sold them. The purchaser afterward refused to pay for them, on the ground that Anderson had destroyed their value by virtually warring against slavery. At this period the feeling in many parts of the South was strong against South Carolina.

This was particularly the case among the young men of Georgia, who looked upon the leaders of secession in the Palmetto State as very presuming, because these leaders thought and acted as if they were the only representatives of Southern sentiment, and as if the leadership belonged to them as a matter of right. They seemed to consider that the mere fact of being born in South Carolina (or Carolina, as they called it, contemptuously ignoring North Carolina) constituted in itself a patent of nobility; and their implied scorn of other States caused the antagonistic feeling which I have mentioned.

This was shared by Anderson, until he found that Georgia also would certainly secede. He then seemed to lose all interest in the Union, and merely desired to become a spectator of the contest, and not an actor. His efforts thenceforth were simply confined to making his fort secure against an assault. Hardly any amount of provocation could induce him to become the assailant.

On the day we left Fort Moultrie, Captain Humphreys, of the engineers, arrived there from Washington, with orders for Captain Foster from the Secretary of War. I have never learned the purport of these dispatches.

On the 27th, the day after we evacuated the place, Lieutenant-colonel Wilmot G. De Saussure arrived at Fort Moultrie, at 9 p.m., with his battalion of Charleston artillery and thirty riflemen; in all, one hundred and seventy men. (The companies composing the battalion were the Marion Artillery, the La Fayette Artillery, the German Artillery, and the Washington Artillery.) I was informed by a spectator that the new-comers were exceedingly cautious in making an entrance. They were looking out for mines in all directions, and had brought ladders with them, on the supposition that there might be torpedoes in front of the main gates. It was a clear, beautiful evening, and the moon was at the full. They were greatly enraged to find the flag-staff cut down, for they had hoped to run up their own flag on the very spot where ours had formerly waved.

They found, too, the gun-carriages burned, and the guns, which had gradually settled down as the carriages gave way, resting with their breeches on the platforms, and the muzzles leaning against the walls. Out of the mouth of each hung a small white string. As many of the guns had been kept loaded for a considerable length of time, these strings had been tied by me to the cartridges, in order that the latter might be pulled out and sunned occasionally, as a precaution against dampness. De Saussure's men imagined that these strings were arranged with a view to blow up the guns the moment any one attempted to interfere with them, and each soldier, as he passed, avoided the supposed danger.

The South Carolina officers, at this period, spent much of their time in discussing military problems. One of these, which was afterward referred to us for solution, occasioned us much amusement. All cannon-balls used in the army, and exposed to the weather, are coated with a varnish of coal-tar, to protect them from rust. Many of those we left behind were in piles near the guns, and when the carriages were burned, the tar melted, ran down in streams, and coagulated in lumps. It was immediately reported that before leaving we had taken great pains to tar the balls, to render them useless.

The problem which puzzled the military *savans* of Charleston was, to determine in what way cannon-balls were ruined by tar. Some months afterward, when we evacuated Fort Sumter, one of the officers who had been much interested in this subject took Seymour aside, and asked him confidentially if he had any objection to tell him why we tarred our balls, assuring him most earnestly that they could scrape it all off.

Upon occupying Fort Sumter, we found it was in a very unfinished condition, and that it would require an immense amount of labour to render it safe against an assault. It had no flanking defences whatever. Three or four hundred men, with short ladders, could easily have taken it; for no guns were mounted, except a few on the gorge, and all the embrasures were open, there being no efficient means of closing them. On the gorge side, where the wharf was located, there were two sally-ports and numerous windows to be guarded. In the second story the embrasures were nothing but large unfinished openings, slightly boarded up. Three or four blows of an axe would have made a broad entrance for an escalading party. The form of the fort was a pentagon. Retaining a small force as a reserve in the centre of the work, we could only furnish eight men to defend each side and guard all the numerous openings.

Fortunately no assault was made. It was thought the fort was almost impregnable, and that there would be no difficulty in inducing Buchanan to order us back to Fort Moultrie. This occasioned a delay, and gave us time to strengthen our position. We were hard at work, mounting guns, preparing shells to be used as hand-grenades, stopping up surplus embrasures, and removing the *débris* which encumbered the passages from one part of the work to another. Quarters were selected for the officers, soldiers, and camp-women; and the household furniture which belonged to each, and which had been thrown pell-mell on the parade-ground, was all separated and deposited in the different rooms. I chose an apartment near the mess hall, and made it so comfortable that Anderson and Seymour came there temporarily to live with me. Our mess was also organized, and placed in charge of Mr. Edward Moale.

In the afternoon, Governor Pickens sent Colonel J.J. Petigru and Major Elison Capers, both field-officers of the rifle regiment, in full uniform, to interview Major Anderson. Their looks were full of wrath, and they bowed stiffly and indignantly in answer to our smiling salutations. I was present at the conversation that ensued, but did not take notes. They told the major that perhaps he was not aware that an agreement had been entered into with President Buchanan not to re-enforce the forts in the harbour. They desired to call his attention to the fact that his recent movement was in direct violation of the contract referred to.

They were, therefore, directed by the governor to request him, peremptorily but courteously, to immediately return to Fort Moultrie. Anderson replied, in substance, that he knew nothing of any such agreement; that as commander of the defences of Charleston he had an inherent right to occupy any fort in the harbour. He stated that he, too, was a Southern man; that he believed the whole difficulty was brought on by the faithlessness of the North—here the aids made a stiff bow—but as regards returning to Fort Moultrie, he could not, and he would not, do it. The commissioners were then courteously dismissed.

I have always felt that this was a most insolent demand. If the governor considered himself aggrieved by our change of station, his redress lay in an appeal to Washington. This attempt to assume command of us, and order us out of a United States fort, was an assumption of authority that merited a more spirited reply.

Before his messengers left, I took occasion, in conversation with a person who came over in the boat with them, to refer to the great strength of the work, and I also spoke of the shells which we had prepared to throw down on the heads of an attacking party. I knew the conversation would be repeated, and hoped it might have some effect in deterring an immediate assault.

A new outrage now took place in full view of our garrison. The United States revenue-cutter, which lay anchored in the stream, was turned over by its commander, Captain N.L. Coste, to the authorities of South Carolina. The previous seizures, made without a declaration of war, had been justified on the ground that the forts and public buildings were fixtures within the limits of the State. To retain this vessel was simply an act of piracy.

When it became apparent that South Carolina did not control the Administration in Washington, and that Anderson would not be ordered back, it is possible a boat attack might have been organized against us; but a storm came up about this time, and the wind was so violent that no small boat could venture out with safety. This occasioned still further delay, which enabled us to do much toward placing the fort in a better condition for defence.

CHAPTER 6

Effect Of Anderson's Movement

Anderson's movement and the sudden uprising of the North put an end to the mission of the South Carolina commissioners. Governor Pickens seized Castle Pinckney and Fort Moultrie on the 27th, and the custom-house and other United States property on the 28th. Before leaving, the commissioners made a formal call upon the President. The latter expected some apology or explanation in relation to the high-handed outrages which had been perpetrated. Had they temporized, or even used conciliatory language on this occasion, it is possible the South might still have preserved the ascendancy it had always held in the councils of the President.

Fortunately, they assumed an air of injured innocence, and required Mr. Buchanan to humble himself before them for the past, and give guarantees for the future by immediately ordering Fort Sumter to be vacated; that is, by surrendering to the State all public property in Charleston Harbor which had not been already stolen. For once, the President, whose personal integrity was called in question, was thoroughly roused, and made the only answer which suited the circumstances. He ordered a man-of-war to proceed to Charleston immediately, drive the State garrisons out of the forts, and take possession of the city. He might, indeed, have arrested the commissioners for high treason; but his Unionism was of a very mild type, and far from being aggressive.

One of the commissioners, Mr. Adams, hastened to telegraph to the authorities of Charleston, on the 28th, to prepare for war immediately, as there were no longer any hopes of a peaceful settlement.

This dispatch caused a great uproar and excitement in Charleston. The banks at once suspended specie payments. All was terror and confusion, for it was expected that a fleet would bombard the city and land troops, and there were no adequate means of opposing its entrance. Castle Pinckney, indeed, might offer some resistance, but as it had been a dependency of Fort Sumter, and unoccupied, little, if any, ammunition was kept there. The governor rushed frantically down to Fort Moultrie to hasten the preparations for defence.

Non-combatants were urged to leave Moultrieville at once. The labourers formerly employed by Captain Foster were again hired by the State engineers, and were kept at work thereafter, night and day, in piling up sand-bags to shield the troops from the fire of Fort Sumter. The batteries at the north-eastern extremity of Sullivan's Island, which were made up of a few old field-pieces brought from the Citadel Academy in the city, were hastily put in order to protect the entrance by that channel. As for Fort Moultrie, before we left we had rendered its armament useless. At this time the guns were still spiked, and the workshops in the city were going night and day to replace the guncarriages that had been burned. In place of these, some of the guns and carriages were sent over from Castle Pinckney.

No attempt had been made to fortify the Morris Island channel, and vessels could enter there without the slightest difficulty. It took several days to transfer the guns and make the preparations I have mentioned. It follows, therefore, that if the Administration had acted promptly, Charleston could have been taken at once, and full reparation exacted for all the wrongs perpetrated against the United States. Why this was not done will be explained hereafter.

Foster had not been able to settle with all his workmen, and the rebels frequently sent them over under a flag of truce to demand their back pay and act as spies. I was enabled through this channel to keep up a correspondence with my wife, who was still in Moultrieville. I learned all that was going on there, and took occasion to inform her that we had no means of lighting up our quarters—a serious inconvenience in those long winter nights. She purchased a gross of matches and a box of candles, and had them put on board one of the boats referred to, in full view of a rebel sentinel, who was supervising the embarkation. She then requested one of the crew, an old soldier named M'Narhamy, who formerly belonged to my company, to deliver them to me, which he agreed to do. The sentinel stared, but the self-possessed manner in which she acted made him think it must be all right, and he did not interfere. The box arrived safely, and added very much to our comfort and convenience.

When the governor found that the spell of Southern supremacy was broken, and that there was no probability that we would be ordered back to Fort Moultrie, he was in a very angry mood. He stopped our mail for a time, and cut off all communication with us. We were, of course, prevented from purchasing fresh provisions, and reduced to pork, beans, and hard-tack. Anderson was quite indignant at this proceeding, and again talked of shutting up the port by putting out the lights in the light-houses.

While the leaders in the city complained bitterly to the public of Anderson for his perfidy in occupying Fort Sumter, they did not hesitate, among themselves, to express their admiration for his acuteness in evading the dangers and difficulties which surrounded him, and for the skilful manner in which he had accomplished it.

Our life now proved to be one of great hardship. Captain Seymour and myself were the only officers for duty as officers of the day, Lieutenant Davis and Lieutenant Hall serving under us as officers of the guard. The situation required constant vigilance. Lieutenant Talbot, being a great sufferer from lung-disease, was unable to do this kind of duty. We were, therefore, very busy during the day superintending measures for defence, and were obliged to be on the alert, and wide awake every other night, so that we were completely exhausted in a short time. Assistant-surgeon Crawford, having no sick in hospital, generously offered to do duty as officer of the day, and his offer was gladly accepted. The two young engineer officers, Snyder and Meade, were also willing to serve as line officers; but Captain Foster thought it was contrary to precedent, and they were not detailed.

As the Engineer department is regarded in this country as the highest branch of the military service, and as its officers are really very able men, I cannot conceive what induced them to build Fort Sumter without any flanking defences whatever, and without fire-proof quarters for the officers. The first defect I endeavoured to remedy by projecting iron-plated, bullet-proof galleries over the angles of the parapet. I left small trap-doors in the bottom of these, for the purpose of throwing down shells on the heads of any party below attempting to force an entrance through the embrasures.

The other defect—the presence of so much combustible matter in the quarters—it was impossible to remedy, and it ultimately cost the loss of the fort. The excuse that it never could have been anticipated that the fort would be attacked from the land side is hardly a valid one, for a foreign fleet might possibly have effected a landing on Morris Island; or they might have set fire to the quarters from the decks of the vessels by means of incendiary shells.

As may well be supposed, there was a great deal of excitement in New York in relation to us; and, in view of the small number of men available for service in the regular army, three of the principal citizens, James A. Hamilton, Moses H. Grinnell, and I.E. Williams, offered, at their own expense, about the last of December, to send us four hundred picked artillerists from the citizen soldiery of the city; but General Scott refused to entertain the proposition.

On the 1st of January, 1861, we took an account of our resources, and found we had but one month's supply of fuel for cooking purposes, but few candles, and no soap. There was, however, a small light-house inside the fort, and we found a little oil stored there.

It seemed to me that the time had now come when forbearance ceased to be a virtue. Even our opponents were willing to acknowledge that we represented a legitimate government, and that both duty and propriety called upon us to resist the numerous war measures which the governor of South Carolina had inaugurated. He had taken forcible possession of two United States forts, of the money in the custom-house, of the custom-house itself, and of other national property in Charleston. He had closed the harbour, by destroying the costly prismatic lenses in the light-houses, and by withdrawing the warning light-ship from Rattlesnake Shoal. He had cut off all communication between us and the city, and had seized the United States mails.

His steamboats, laden with war material to be used in erecting batteries against us, were allowed to pass and repass Fort Sumter, not only without opposition, but without even a protest. Worse than all, he had commenced imprisoning the crews of merchant vessels for contumacy in refusing to acknowledge his authority as the head of an independent nation. In vain did these vessels reverse their flags in a mute appeal to us to use our guns in their defence. Anderson would do nothing—not even send a communication to the governor on the subject, although the latter, without authority from the State Legislature, was thus wielding all the powers of a military dictator.

The enemy were greatly emboldened at our weakness or timidity, and with good reason, for they saw us stand by with folded arms, and allow steamboat loads of ammunition and war material to pass us, on their way to Morris Island, to be used in the erection and arming of batteries to prevent any United States vessels from coming to our assistance.

Major Anderson was neither timid nor irresolute, and he was fully aware of his duties and responsibilities. Unfortunately, he desired not only to save the Union, but to save slavery with it. Without this, he considered the contest as hopeless. In this spirit he submitted to everything, and delayed all action in the expectation that Congress would make some new and more binding compromise which would restore peace to the country. He could not read the signs of the times, and see that the conscience of the nation and the progress of civilization had already doomed slavery to destruction. If he had taken this view of the situation, he would have made more strenuous efforts to hold on to the harbour of Charleston, and the one hundred and twenty millions of dollars, more or less, spent to regain it might still have formed part of the national treasury.

The applause which, both in the North and South, greeted his masterly movement of the 26th of December, made him feel more like an arbiter between two contending nations than a simple soldier engaged in carrying out the instructions of his superiors. To show the spirit in which he acted, it is only necessary to quote from his letter to Governor Pickens while the rebellion was still pending. He wrote: "My dear Governor, my heart was never in this war." This sentiment was repeated by him in letters to other parties, and, strange to say, was actually sent in the form of an official communication to the adjutant-general of the army.

The difficulties he experienced in his unavailing attempts to defer hostilities seriously impaired his health and spirits, and ultimately brought on the disease which kept him almost entirely out of service during the remainder of the war, and in all probability hastened his death.

However much I differed from him in regard to his pro-slavery sentiments, I take pleasure in stating that, aside from his political career, the graces of his private life were such as to win the esteem and regard of all who knew him.

CHAPTER 7

The *Star Of The West*

About the close of the year a great fear fell upon Charleston, for they had received positive information that a United States naval vessel was on its way to the city. The President had indeed acted promptly. On the 31st of December, he ordered the *Brooklyn*, man-of-war, under Captain Farragut, to take three hundred veteran soldiers on board from Fortress Monroe, as a re-enforcement for us, and then proceed to Charleston Harbor to drive out the State troops, and resume possession of the public property. General Scott, the commander-in-chief, assented to the arrangement at the time; but, unfortunately, he was afterward seized with doubts as to whether the withdrawing of so many men from Fortress Monroe might not endanger its safety; and that being a far more important work than Fort Sumter, he did not like to run any risk in relation to it.

He therefore induced Mr. Buchanan to change the order, and substitute for the *Brooklyn* a merchant vessel, loaded with supplies and two hundred and fifty recruits.[1] This was a fatal error, for the steamer chosen, the *Star of the West*, was, from its nature, wholly unfitted to contend with shore batteries. The general, who at this time was quite pacifically inclined, may have thought that if this vessel could slip in, and land its cargo unawares, he would have secured the harbour of Charleston without increasing the war fever in the South. Be this as it may, there is no doubt that his policy was too peaceful in the early days of the war.

1 The facts in this statement are taken from Dawson's *Historical Magazine for January, 1872*

When a company of the most distinguished men in Washington was formed, under Cassius M. Clay, to prevent the capture of the President, and the destruction of the public buildings, he gave positive orders to Senator Nye, who was on duty at the Navy-yard, not to fire upon the enemy in case they came there to take possession.

The original plan to succour us was excellent: the substitute was an utter failure. A change of this kind always occasions more or less delay, and in the present instance nearly a week elapsed before the vessel left New York. The enemy took immediate advantage of the time thus gained, to put up a work to control the main channel which passes by Morris Island, and which had previously been wholly unobstructed. They received the telegraphic notice on the 31st of December that a man-of-war would be sent, and the very next day the cadets of the Citadel Academy were hard at work at the new battery. It was located so that it would command the channel, and at the same time be beyond the reach of our guns. The day was cold and rainy, and the wind blew fiercely. We wondered how long those boys would keep up their enthusiasm amidst the hardships and trials of the real war which was now fast approaching.

Our chaplain, who had been present at the raising of the flag, and had then returned to his family in Moultrieville, desired to make us another visit. For this purpose, he called upon the rebel commander at Fort Moultrie, and asked if there would be any obstacle thrown in the way of his crossing over to see us. The answer was, "Oh no, parson; I think I will give you a pass."

The chaplain replied, "I did not ask you for a pass, sir! I am a United States officer, and I shall visit a United States fort whenever I think proper, without asking your permission. I simply desire to know whether you intend to prevent my going by force." He was not allowed to cross; and as he soon gave new proofs of contumacy by persisting in praying for the President of the United States, when asked to hold services in the chapel, before the rebel soldiers, he was soon banished, and his property confiscated.

The ladies we had left behind naturally felt a strong-desire to be with us once more. My wife did not wish to ask permission of the rebel authorities, and I saw little chance of her coming in any other way. Nevertheless, to my surprise, she made her appearance at the wharf at Fort Sumter on the afternoon of the 3rd of January. It seems she found a boat-load of labourers about to make the passage, for the purpose of obtaining their back pay from Captain Foster. She took a seat in the stern of the boat, and told them to take her with them. The sentinel who was there to examine the passes did not interfere or ask her any questions, so she came over without difficulty. Mrs. Foster and her sister, Mrs. Smith, were already with us, having obtained a permit from the governor. Mrs. Seymour had made an unsuccessful application to the commander of Fort Moultrie, and had been somewhat rudely refused. Two clever little boys, sons of our generous-hearted sutler, Dan Sinclair, volunteered to row her across. After dark, they pulled a boat out from under a house up the beach; and as there was no guard there, Mrs. Seymour came over without difficulty.

The ladies were desirous of remaining an indefinite length of time; but we had no means of making them comfortable, and Major Anderson thought their presence would merely add to our embarrassment. In accordance with his wishes, they left that night and the next day. The cold was intense, and as all the wood was retained for cooking purposes, I was obliged to split up a mahogany table for fuel, to keep my wife from suffering during her brief visit. She and Mrs. Seymour went back with the Sinclair boys at midnight. They succeeded in making a landing, and in reaching the chaplain's house without being observed.

In the mean time, an amusing scene had occurred there. A very chivalrous gentleman, Ex-Governor Means, of South Carolina, had learned in some way that Mrs. Seymour had been rudely refused permission to visit her husband in Fort Sumter. He thought this action of the commandant of Fort Moultrie harsh and unnecessary, and was kind enough to take the trouble to call at the chaplain's house to assure Mrs. Seymour that he would procure her a pass from higher authority. The chaplain hardly knew how to act. He did not like to tell the ex-governor that Mrs. Seymour had already gone, for fear it might get the Sinclair boys into trouble.

He therefore pretended that Mrs. Seymour was confined to her room with a sick-headache. The ex-governor sent in repeated messages to beg that she would see him, if it was only for a moment, but the answers made up by Mrs. Harris were invariably in the negative. The chaplain afterward laughed heartily at the equivocal position he had been forced to assume.

Now that we were alone once more, we went to work with a will. The Baltimore labourers were of inestimable value. They did an immense amount of labour in the way of mounting guns, and moving weighty materials from one part of the work to another; but they showed no inclination to take part in the fighting, should any occur.

On the 3d, the South Carolina commissioners finally shook off the dust from their feet, and left Washington, having utterly failed to accomplish the object of their mission.

On the same day, the governor, through Mr. Gourdin's[2] influence, permitted us to receive our mails once more. By this date we had mounted all the guns we were able to man on the lower tier, and had bricked up the surplus windows, sally-ports, and embrasures, as we had no one to guard them. The enemy, in the mean time, had erected a battery at Fort Johnson, and marked out another directly opposite to us in Moultrieville.

On the 6th, the mayor of New York, Fernando Wood, promulgated a message to the effect that the Union was breaking up, and recommending that the city of New York secede from the State. At this time the seeming indifference of the politicians to our fate made us feel like orphan children of the Republic, deserted by both the State and Federal administrations.

On the same day, Governor Pickens graciously allowed Mrs. Anderson to visit her husband, but coupled the permission with the ungenerous stipulation that the interview must take place in presence of witnesses. He disliked very much to disoblige her, as she belonged to one of the most distinguished families of Geor-

---

2. One of the original leaders of secession, and a life-long friend and correspondent of Major Anderson

gia, and had many influential relatives among the Secessionists.

Mr. Gourdin too, who was a warm personal friend of her husband, exerted himself in her behalf. While she herself displayed great patriotism, several of her brothers in the final attack on Fort Sumter were on the opposite side, fighting against her husband. Under the circumstances, her visit to us was a brief one. She brought a valuable addition to the fort in the shape of Peter Hart, a gallant and trustworthy man, who had been Anderson's orderly sergeant in Mexico. She felt much easier in her mind, now that the major had Hart to look after him. He was only permitted to join us on condition that his duties were to be those of a civilian, and not of a soldier.

On the 8th, the governor, who, like Louis XIV., might very readily have said, "*L'état, c'est moi!*" concluded to form a cabinet to assist him in his onerous duties. He accordingly appointed J.G. Magrath Secretary of State; D.F. Jamison, Secretary of War; C.G. Memminger, Secretary of the Treasury; A.C. Garlington, Secretary of the Interior; and W.H. Harlee, Postmaster-general.

On the same day, our ladies, who had assembled at the Mills House, in Charleston, left for the North in a body, on account of the state of public feeling in the city.[3]

Their presence with us threw a momentary brightness over the scene, but after their departure everything looked more gloomy and disheartening than before. The fort itself was a deep, dark, damp, gloomy-looking place, inclosed in high walls, where the sunlight rarely penetrated. If we ascended to the parapet, we saw nothing but uncouth State flags, representing palmettos, pelicans, and other strange devices. No echo seemed to come back from the loyal North to encourage us. Our glasses in vain swept the horizon; the one flag we longed to see was not there. It did come at last, in a timid, apologetic way, and not as a representative of the war power of the Government.

We had seen a statement in a Northern paper that a steam-

3. My wife applied for board in Charleston, but was told she must first obtain the sanction of Mr. Rhett, the editor of the *Mercury*. She was afterward informed by the boarding-house keeper that, as the house depended on the patronage of the Southern people for support, she (the landlady) could not undertake to harbour the wives of Federal officers.

er named the *Star of the West*, which belonged to Marshall O. Roberts, was to be sent to us, under command of Captain John M`Gowan, with a re-enforcement of several hundred men and supplies of food and ammunition; but we could not credit the rumour. To publish all the details of an expedition of this kind, which ought to be kept a profound secret, was virtually telling South Carolina to prepare her guns to sink the vessel. It was hard to believe the Government would send to us a mercantile steamer—a mere transport, utterly unfitted to contend with shore batteries—when it could dispatch a man-of-war furnished with all the means and appliances to repel force by force.

As the insurgents at this period had but few field-guns, and a very scanty supply of cannon-powder, the *Brooklyn* alone, in my opinion, could have gone straight to the wharf in Charleston, and have put an end to the insurrection then and there; for we all know what its distinguished captain, Farragut, was able to accomplish when left to his own resources.

It seems, however, the news was literally true. The expedition was fitted out by Lieutenant Washington A. Bartlett, an ex-officer of our navy.[4] Although I had little faith in the announcement, I scanned with increased interest every vessel that approached the harbour.

Soon after daylight, on the morning of the 9th, I was on the parapet with my spy-glass; for I fancied, from a signal I had observed the previous evening on a pilot-boat, that something must be coming. As I looked seaward, I saw a large steamer pass the bar and enter the Morris Island channel. It had the ordinary United States flag up; and as it evidently did not belong to the navy, I came to the conclusion it must be the *Star of the West*. I do not remember that any other officers were on the lookout at this time. Anderson himself was still in bed. When the vessel came opposite the new battery, which had just been built by the cadets, I saw a shot fired to bring her to.

Soon after this an immense United States garrison-flag was

---

4. The army officers on board were First Lieutenant Charles R. Woods, Ninth Infantry, commanding; First Lieutenant William A. Webb, Fifth Infantry; Second Lieutenant Charles W. Thomas, First Infantry; and Assistant-surgeon P.G.S. Ten Broeck.

run up at the fore. Without waiting to ascertain the result of the firing, I dashed down the back stairs to Anderson's room, to notify him of the occurrence. He told me to have the long roll beaten, and to post the men at the guns on the parapet. I ran out, called the drummers, and had the alarm sounded. It took but a few minutes for men and officers to form at the guns in readiness for action. The battery was still firing, but the transport had passed by, and was rapidly getting out of range.

At the same time it was approaching within gun-shot of Fort Moultrie. The latter immediately opened fire from one or two guns. Anderson would not allow us to return this fire; and the captain of the vessel, wholly discouraged by our failure to respond, turned about, and made his way back to New York. Two shots had struck the steamer, but no essential injury was done. I think the people in Fort Moultrie, who expected to be driven out to take refuge behind the sand-hills, were especially astonished at our inaction. It is very true that the Morris Island battery was beyond the reach of our guns.

Still, we did not know this positively at the time; and our firing in that direction, even if ineffectual, would have encouraged the steamer to keep on its course. We had one or two guns bearing on Fort Moultrie; and as that was within easy range, we could have kept down the fire there long enough to enable the steamer to come in. It was plainly our duty to do all that we could. For anything we knew to the contrary, she might have been in a sinking condition. Had she gone down before our eyes, without an effort on our part to aid her, Anderson would have incurred a fearful responsibility by his inaction.

Mr. Dawson, in his account of these incidents in the *Historical Magazine*, has it that a council of war was held by us to determine whether we would fire or not, and that we decided not to fire. He founds this upon verbal statements made by Foster and Davis. I know Foster was under this impression; but upon my recalling the circumstances to his recollection a short time before his death, he admitted his mistake. My memory is very clear and distinct on this point, and I am sustained in regard to it by both Seymour and Crawford. Davis I have not seen for some time, but I have no doubt he will confirm what I have said when his memory is refreshed.

Indeed there was no time for deliberation while the troops were at the guns, for the vessel was moving very rapidly, and the whole affair was over in a few minutes. The council was held after the steamer had gone, to determine what action ought to be taken in consequence of the attack. It was too late then for resistance, and all we could do was to send Lieutenant Hall to the governor with a flag of truce, to demand an explanation. In this communication, Anderson expressly stated that if he did not receive a satisfactory reply, he would not, hereafter, allow any vessel from Charleston to pass within reach of his guns. As might be expected, the governor replied that he took the responsibility of the firing, and would do it again under like circumstances.

Anderson then reconvened the council to lay this answer before them. Through his influence it was concluded to send Lieutenant Talbot to Washington with a full statement of the occurrence, and await his return with specific instructions from the War Department. To carry out even this programme, the major was obliged to obtain the governor's permission for Lieutenant Talbot to pass through Charleston. It was urged by Anderson that the delay would enable us to finish our preparations for defence; but it was evident that time was far more valuable to the enemy than it was to us, for it enabled them to complete and arm their batteries, and close the harbour against our men-of-war, thus virtually imprisoning us in our island home.

When Talbot left, we resumed our labours as usual. No attempt was made to carry out the threat of stopping all passing vessels.

By the 14th of January our heavy guns were up; but by that time, too, the greater part of Fort Moultrie and Castle Pinckney were shielded from our direct fire by huge piles of sand-bags.[5]

---

5. Castle Pinckney at this time was commanded by Colonel J. Johnston Petigru; Sullivan's Island, by Adjutant and Inspector-general Dunovant; Fort Johnson, by Captain James Johnson, of the Charleston Rifles. The United States Arsenal, by Colonel John Cunningham, of the Seventeenth South Carolina militia; its former commander, Captain Humphreys, the United States military store-keeper, having been ejected on the 30th of December.

We now began to get out of fuel, but we still had a resource in some wooden sheds inside the fort, which had been used as a temporary shelter for cement and building materials. Our position was greatly alleviated in one respect. Owing, it is said, to the influence of Mr. Gourdin, already referred to as a leading Secessionist, and an old friend of Major Anderson, we were allowed to receive our mails once more. After the *Star of the West* affair, they probably thought we were very harmless people, and deserved some reward for our forbearance.

CHAPTER 8

A Resort to Diplomacy

And now the Charleston statesmen concocted a plan to take away from us all hope of succour, so that we might be induced to surrender. To this end they determined to fill up the entrance of the harbour by depositing stone there. Whether they really intended to do this, or made a pretence of doing it, I never knew; but they certainly did obtain some old hulks from Savannah, and sunk them in the channel. Either these hulks were deposited in the wrong places, or else the tide drifted them into deep water, for it is certain they never formed any impediment to navigation afterward. Perhaps it was a mere *coup de théâtre*, to intimidate us, and prevent re-enforcements from attempting to come in; at all events, it was a preliminary to a grand effort to negotiate us out of Fort Sumter.

For this purpose two representative men came over from the city on the 11th, in the little steamer *Antelope*, under a white flag. The party consisted of the late United States district judge, A.G. Magrath, now Secretary of State for South Carolina, and General D.F. Jamison, their new Secretary of War. The judge, who was the champion orator of the State, made a long and eloquent speech, the purport of which was that South Carolina was determined to have Fort Sumter at all hazards; that they would pull it down with their fingernails, if they could not get it in any other way; that the other Southern States were becoming excited on the subject; that President Buchanan was in his dotage; that the government in Washington was breaking up; that all was confusion, despair, and disorder there; and that it was full time for us to look out for our own safety, for if we refused to give up the fort nothing could prevent the Southern troops from exterminating us. He ended this tragical statement by saying, "May God Almighty enable you to come to a just decision!"

Anderson seemed deeply affected at the prospect of hostilities. He asked them why they did not first attempt diplomacy, instead of war. He said if they would send a commissioner to lay their claims before the authorities at Washington, he would send another to represent the condition of the fort; and the Government could then form its own judgment, and come to some decision. Judge Magrath replied that he would report the proposition to Governor Pickens for his action. He and his companion then took a solemn leave of us, and returned to Charleston.

Upon reporting the facts to the governor, it was at once decided to accept Anderson's proposition. They gained an immense advantage in so doing; for the agreement tied the hands of the United States for an indefinite period of time, and prevented the arrival of any war vessels until South Carolina was fully prepared to receive them. The delay gave the State time to complete and man its batteries, and to obtain an unlimited number of guns and quantities of shot and shell from the cannon foundry at Richmond, Virginia, known as the Tredegar Iron Works. Thus, while our supplies would be running out, theirs would be coming in.

Every day's delay would weaken us and strengthen them. I was strongly opposed to this fatal measure, which ultimately cost us the loss of Fort Sumter; but as it had simply emanated from Anderson himself, by virtue of his powers as commanding officer, and had not been submitted to a council of war, there was no opportunity for protest. He was at this time at the height of his popularity, and everything he did was sure to be sustained at Washington.

In this embassy, Colonel Isaac W. Hayne, an eminent lawyer of Charleston, was chosen as the commissioner from South Carolina, and Lieutenant Norman J. Hall was sent as a representative of Fort Sumter.

After this event everything went on, for a while, as usual.

By the 15th of January we had secured the main gates against an assault, by building a wall of stone and mortar behind them, leaving merely what is called a man-hole, for the entrance of one person at a time. Even this was covered by a twenty-four-pounder howitzer, loaded with canister.

By the 11th the money appropriated by the South Carolina Legislature for war purposes amounted to $1,450,000, and was soon after increased to $1,800,000. There was not a dollar in the treasury, and nothing but the bank of the State to draw upon.

On the same day the financial condition of the United States was much improved by the appointment of John A. Dix as Secretary of the Treasury. This gave great confidence to the moneyed men of New York, who immediately rallied to the support of the Government.

To all appearance, about six hundred negroes were now at work, night and day, in perfecting the defences of Fort Moultrie. The enemy continued their hostile preparations with the utmost energy and zeal, in spite of the tacit truce which was supposed to exist, and which prevented the President from sending men-of-war to aid or to re-enforce us. I think Anderson might well have remonstrated against the landing of additional heavy guns and mortars on Sullivan's Island, and the erection or new batteries, to be used against us. He should at once have reported this increased activity to Washington, in order that the agreement might be terminated, or at least limited to a certain number of days.

On the 17th, Judge Holt was nominated as Secretary of War, and was soon after confirmed by the Senate. We were very glad to have an energetic and patriotic man at the head of this department.

On the 18th, Lieutenant Meade left us for his home in Richmond, Virginia, in consequence of a dispatch which stated that his mother was at the point of death. I never knew whether this telegram was founded on fact, or was a strategic move to force poor Meade into the ranks of the Confederacy, by detaching him temporarily from us, and taking him where tremendous political and social influences could be brought to bear upon him. He had previously been overwhelmed with letters on the subject.

He was already much troubled in mind; and some months after the bombardment of Fort Sumter the pressure of family ties induced him (very reluctantly, as I heard) to join the Disunionists. It was stated that he never was a happy man afterward, and that before a year had passed death put an end to his sorrow and regret. He was the son of R.K. Meade, our minister to Brazil.

The troops opposite to us were now regularly receiving supplies and re-enforcements, and drilling daily, while all the necessaries of life were constantly diminishing with us. We were already out of sugar, soap, and candles.

On the 19th, Lieutenant Talbot returned from his visit to Washington, where, it will be remembered, he had been sent to explain the *Star of the West* affair, and ask for specific instructions, which would relieve Anderson from the responsibility, and throw it upon the Administration. The orders he brought back were to the effect that they had the utmost confidence in Major Anderson, and that they left everything to his judgment. This was throwing the responsibility all back upon him. It was very complimentary, but far from satisfactory.

Talbot stated that he had great difficulty in making a safe transit through Charleston; for while the leaders seemed to be more pacific than ever, the populace had become more violent. It was even thought necessary to send an officer with him to secure his personal safety. He brought me the pleasant information that the mob were howling for my head, as that of the only Republican, or, as they called it, "Black Republican," in the fort.

Many unfavourable comments having been made, even in the Southern States, more particularly in Kentucky, in relation to Governor Pickens's treatment of us, he relaxed his severity, and on the 21st sent us over some fresh beef and vegetables; as if we would consent to be fed by the charity of South Carolina. Anderson showed a good deal of proper spirit on this occasion. He declined to receive the provisions, but notified the governor that, if we were not interfered with, we would purchase our own supplies in Charleston market. The governor consented to this;

but nothing came of it.

There seemed to be a combination among the market-men not to sell us any food. Indeed, this action of the governor made him very unpopular with the Rhett faction. Rhett rushed over to inform him that the people demanded that Fort Sumter should be taken without any further procrastination or delay. The governor made a very shrewd reply. He said, "Certainly, Mr. Rhett; I have no objection! I will furnish you with some men, and you can storm the work yourself." Rhett drew back and replied, "But, sir, I am not a military man!" "Nor I either," said the governor, "and therefore I take the advice of those that are!" After this, there was no further talk of an immediate assault. The action of the governor in this case almost gained him the reputation of a wit among the officers of his command.

Lieutenant Hall being absent on diplomatic duty, and Dr. Crawford being temporarily, and Lieutenant Talbot permanently, on the sick-list, the rest of us were utterly worn out with the labour that devolved upon us. Guard duty was especially severe, as increased vigilance became necessary, in consequence of certain threatening preparations made by the enemy. The leaders in Charleston soon saw that the joint mission of Hall and Hayne could not possibly result in any thing decisive; but as every day added to their strength and resources, they did not choose to recall their commissioner.

They left him to continue his arguments in relation to the "right of eminent domain," while they prepared for war. In the hope that someday they might take us by surprise, they had the guard-boats, which still patrolled the harbour, painted black, and all the lights and fires carefully screened from view. They probably intended to choose a dark night to drop down noiselessly with the tide, and take advantage of a sleepy sentinel, or some other favourable circumstance, to land a party on the rocks at the base of the wall, and seize the main entrance, or make their way in through one of the embrasures.

On the 24th, New York City, speaking through its mayor, Fernando Wood, seemed to offer the right hand of fellowship to the Secessionists. Certain arms which had been purchased by Georgia, to be used against the General Government, were detained in New York, and Ex-Senator Toombs telegraphed to Wood for an explanation. The latter characterized the detention as an outrage for which he was not responsible, and for which he would inflict summary punishment, if he had the power.

Lieutenant Meade returned faithfully on the 25th, but brought no news of importance.

On the 26th, Anderson applied for the code of naval signals, so that if a fleet at any time should cross the bar, he might communicate with it at a distance.

Up to the 30th we had not been able to procure anything to eat from the city; but through the influence of Mr. Gourdin, who seemed to have a special mission to smooth over all difficulties, a new arrangement was made, by which our provisions were ostensibly purchased for Fort Johnson, and were forwarded to us from there.

The nearest land to us was called Cummings Point. It was nearly opposite the gorge, which was the weakest side of Fort Sumter, the wall there being thinner than in any other part. The enemy now began to build the most formidable of all their batteries on the point referred to. It was constructed of strong timber, plated with railroad iron, and partially covered with sand. When finished, it was regarded as almost impregnable. Steamers from the city passed within a stone's-throw of us daily, loaded with the materials used in its construction, without opposition and without remonstrance.

As it seemed settled that we were to wait until Hayne was through with his law-points, and as our food, in the mean time, was rapidly giving out, Anderson, on the 21st, directed me to make arrangements with the authorities of Charleston to enable us to send off the soldiers' families to Fort Hamilton. This was done; and the women and children were shipped off to Charleston on the 30th, and transferred to the steamer *Marion*, which left for New York on the 3rd of February. As they passed the fort outward-bound, the men gave them repeated cheers as a farewell, and displayed much feeling; for they thought it very probable they might not meet them again for a long period, if ever.[1]

On the arrival of these families at Fort Hamilton, New York, they found themselves in straitened circumstances, because, owing to our isolation, the men had not been paid off for a long time, and therefore had no money to give their wives. Plymouth Church, however, interested itself in their behalf, and soon made them comparatively comfortable.

Had our Government been really disposed, at this period, to act with ordinary energy, it might have opened a communication with us, and cleared the Morris Island channel without much difficulty. There were only about three hundred Charleston militia guarding the batteries on that island; and it would have been easy for a small force of mariners and soldiers to land there in the night, take the batteries in reverse, and drive the troops out, or capture them. This once accomplished, re-enforcements and supplies could have been sent us to any amount. Buchanan's administration, however, was drawing to a close; and his only desire seemed to be to get through his term of office without a collision, leaving the difficulties and perplexities of his position as a legacy to his successor.

On the 30th, I received an insulting letter from Charleston, informing me that, if I were ever caught in the city, an arrangement had been made to tar and feather me as an Abolitionist.

February had now arrived. The 4th of the month was made memorable by the meeting of the Peace Congress at Washington, and by a convention to represent the Southern States at Montgomery, Alabama.

On the 6th, the new Secretary of War, Judge Holt, wrote to South Carolina that the President did not intend to inaugurate

---

1. Among these children was a little waif, called Dick Kowley, afterward known as "Sumter Dick." He had been abandoned by his mother, and thus thrown out on the world. For a time he was sent, after his arrival in New York, to the house of Dr. Stewart, who was a family connection of mine. After supper he reminded the ladies that he had not heard tattoo yet, and wished to know at what hour they beat the reveille. He evidently thought every well-regulated family kept a drummer and fifer on hand, to sound the calls. He was very unhappy until he had procured a small stick and a miniature flag. Every morning at sunrise he hoisted the flag, and carefully lowered it and put it away at sunset. He is now a cabinet-maker at Marion, Ohio, and recently gained a prize for his excellent workmanship.

any aggressive measures; and if the State government attacked Fort Sumter, they would incur a fearful responsibility.

On the 8th, some photographic artists were allowed to come over and take our portraits in a group. I think it proved a profitable speculation, for the sale was quite large. One of the party proved afterward to be a lieutenant of a Charleston company. It seems he came as a spy, and, no doubt, thought he had done a very clever thing; but inasmuch as Mr. Gourdin and other Secessionists, including several military and naval officers, were permitted to roam through the fort at will, there was very little use in taking precautions against spies. Indeed, on one occasion, another Major Anderson, a namesake of our commander, came down to Charleston with a freight-train loaded with shot, shell, heavy guns, and mortars for South Carolina, to be used in the batteries against us.

He was the owner of the celebrated Tredegar Iron Works, of Richmond, Virginia, already referred to, and had been enriched by the patronage of the United States. I thought it decidedly cool in him, under the circumstances, to come over to call on our Major Anderson. He made no attempt at concealment, but stated without reserve the object of his trip to the South. To my surprise, instead of being summarily expelled, he met with a most cordial reception, was invited to stay to dinner, and when he left he was dismissed with a "Goodbye! God bless you! You haven't such a thing as a late newspaper about you, have you?"

On the 9th of February, the enemy's batteries were completed, manned and ready for action. On the same day the Confederate Government was duly organized by the election of Jefferson Davis, of Mississippi, as President, and Alexander H. Stephens, of Georgia, as Vice-president. The Cabinet consisted of Robert Toombs, of Georgia, Secretary of State; L. Pope Walker, of Alabama, Secretary of War; and Charles G. Memminger, of South Carolina, Secretary of the Treasury. Afterward, Judah P. Benjamin, of Louisiana, was appointed Attorney-general; Stephen M. Mallory, of Florida, Secretary of the Navy; and John H. Reagan, of Texas, Postmaster-general. Peter Gustave T. Beauregard, of Louisiana, was made Brigadier-general to command the provisional army.

By this time we had finished most of our preparations, and were busily engaged in constructing a mine at the extremity of the wharf, for the benefit of any hostile party that might land there.

Lieutenant Hall returned on the 10th. He had had a very pleasant time in Washington, and had been petted a good deal by the loyal people of the North, but his mission proved of no real benefit to the United States, and we had missed him a great deal, for we had been very short-handed.

He brought nothing definite from the Administration. All the latter desired was to have a peaceable death-bed, leaving its burdens for Mr. Lincoln's shoulders.

As Hall passed through Charleston, one of the young men there told him there was quite a revulsion of feeling with regard to attacking Fort Sumter. Hall inquired the reason. The reply was, that a schooner which had just come in had been in great danger from one of our infernal machines, which had exploded and whitened the water for three hundred yards around. It seems that Seymour, who is very ingenious, had fastened a cannon cartridge in the centre of a barrel of paving-stones, so arranged that when the barrel was rolled off the parapet, the powder would explode about five feet from the base of the wall. I was trying the experiment one day as the schooner passed, and the explosion did look very destructive, as the paving-stones dashed up the water for a distance of fifty feet from the fort.

On the 14th, we had two more mines ready for any storming party that might desire to land.

About this time Captain Edward M'Cready, of Charleston, who had formerly been very intimate with the officers of the garrison, wrote a letter urging them to throw off their allegiance to the United States, and enter into the Confederate service. No one took the trouble to answer it.

CHAPTER 9

The Crisis at Hand

We saw advertisements now in the Northern papers showing that dramas founded on our occupation of Fort Sumter, and
confinement there, were being acted both in Boston and New
York. It was quite amusing to see our names in the play-bills, and
to find that persons were acting our parts and spouting mock
heroics on the stage.

On the 15th, several Southern senators at Washington wrote
to Governor Pickens, recommending that we be allowed fresh
provisions, fuel, and other necessaries, at the same time expressing their sympathy with South Carolina. After this the governor
became more polite and considerate, and allowed our officers
to send to purchase oil and groceries in Charleston. Rhett's paper, *The Mercury*, of course, bitterly opposed this concession. We
now learned that the whole question of Fort Sumter had been
turned over to the new Southern Confederacy for solution.

At this period grievous complaints were made by the merchants of the city of the utter stagnation of trade. All the business had fled to Savannah. Foreign vessels would not attempt to
enter a harbour where civil war was raging, especially as it was
reported that obstructions had been sunk in the channel. The
Charleston people said they now fully understood and appreciated the kindness of the people of Savannah in furnishing them
with old hulks to destroy the harbour of Charleston.

When the organization of the new government was complete, the original Secessionists of the Palmetto State were exceedingly angry to find themselves ignored. The President, Vice-

president, and all the prominent members of the Cabinet, with the single exception of the Secretary of the Treasury, were from other States. Henceforward, instead of pretentious leadership, the position of South Carolina was to be that of humble obedience to the new *régime*. Nor was this their only grievance. Free trade was not proclaimed; and no ordinance was passed to re-open the African slave-trade, inasmuch as it would destroy the domestic slave-trade and the profits of slave-breeding in Virginia. It was soon seen that the associated States differed widely on a great many vital points.

One of these related to Indian incursions into Texas. The Border States, owing to the withdrawal of the United States forces, desired large appropriations in money, for the purpose of organizing troops to guard the settlements from Indian incursions. The people of South Carolina, whose burdens were already very great, and who were advertising in vain for a loan, were very unwilling to be taxed for the benefit of Texas and Arkansas.

In their anger at these untoward events, the proposition was freely discussed whether it would not be the best course to secede from the Confederacy altogether, and place themselves under a British protectorate. The only difficulty in the way seemed to be the unwillingness of Great Britain to act as step-father to such a spoiled child as South Carolina.

Virginia had not yet seceded. She still professed neutrality, but allowed a brisk trade in cannon and ammunition to be carried on with the South, knowing they were to be used against the General Government.

Anderson now expressed himself as openly opposed to coercion. He was in favour of surrendering all the forts to the States in which they were located. This course would simply be an acknowledgment that the sovereignty did not vest in the United States, and would have led to nothing but disorder and disunion. He said if his native State, Kentucky, seceded, he should throw up his commission and go to Europe. The fact is, as I have stated, he was a strong pro-slavery man, and felt bitterly toward the North for not carrying out the Fugitive Slave Law. He contended that slavery was right in principle, and expressly sanctioned by the Bible. One day, while we were conversing on the subject, I called his attention to the fact that slavery in ancient times was not founded on colour; and if white slavery was right, I saw no reason why someone might not make a slave of him, and read texts of Scripture to him to keep him quiet. He was unable to answer this argument.[1]

On the 1st of March, he informed the General Government that he had no doubt we would soon be attacked. The communication, however, led to no comment and no immediate action.

From certain circumstances, I saw that South Carolina not only intended to build iron-clad batteries, but was thinking of iron-clad ships, to sink our wooden navy, and at some future time capture our Northern Harbors.

I was so much impressed with the importance of this subject that I felt it my duty to call attention to it, in letters to Mr. Curtis, of Missouri, and other members of Congress; but no one at the North seemed to give the matter a second thought, or imagine there was any danger to be apprehended in the future. It was not so with our enemies. They were fully alive to the aggressive power it would give them, and they commenced to experiment by building an iron-clad floating battery, which was to be plated deep enough to resist our heaviest metal. When finished, it was to be anchored off the gorge of Fort Sumter, so that it could beat down our main gates, and make wide breaches in the walls for an assaulting party to enter. This battery was completed on the 3rd of March; but the State militia had a great prejudice against it, and could not be induced to man it. They christened it "The Slaughter Pen," and felt certain it would go to the bottom the moment we opened fire upon it. Out of deference to public opinion, it was tied up to the wharf in Moultrieville, and took part from that position in the final bombardment of Fort Sumter.

The eventful 4th of March had now arrived, and with it a

---

1. It is due to the major to state that, in a speech made before the Board of Brokers in New York, on the 13th of May, he asserted that if the question lay between the preservation of the Union or the preservation of slavery, slavery must be sacrificed.

new President, representing the patriotism and vigour of the great North-west. We looked for an immediate change of policy; but it was some weeks before any definite action was taken with regard to us. This is not to be wondered at, when we consider that a large proportion of the *employés* of the previous Administration were disloyal and treacherous, while the new appointments could not be made hastily, on account of the tremendous pressure for office, and the difficulty of canvassing the claims of so many rival and influential candidates.

If Mr. Lincoln wrote a private dispatch, it was sure to be betrayed to the enemy. The defection in the civil service, in the army, and navy, was so great that, if he gave an order, he was always in doubt whether it would be faithfully carried out. General Cooper, who was adjutant-general of the army, and the mouth-piece of the Secretary of War and of the commander-in-chief, was himself a rebel at heart, and soon resigned to join the Confederacy.

Enough, however, was already known of the policy of the Administration to cause great uneasiness in Charleston. The feeling there was very gloomy at the prospect of real war; for almost everyone had persuaded himself that the new President would not attempt coercion, but would simply submit to the dismemberment of the country, and make the best terms he could. They now knew they would be obliged to face the storm they had raised, and they already foresaw great sufferings and sacrifices in the future.

On the 5th, Anderson wrote to Washington that he needed no re-enforcement. The fact is, he did not want it, because its arrival would be sure to bring on a collision, and that was the one thing he wished to avoid.

Mr. Lincoln soon after appointed Simon Cameron as the new Secretary of War.

On the 7th, an accidental shot, fired from the battery opposite, struck near our wharf. The enemy sent a boat over at once to make an explanation.

Our men were dissatisfied that the affair ended in nothing. They were becoming thoroughly angry and disgusted at their long confinement, and at the supervision South Carolina exercised over them. One and all desired to fight it out as soon as possible.

After consultation with Major Anderson, it was deemed impossible at Washington to succour us without sending a force of at least twenty thousand men to storm the batteries on Morris Island. There was a time when these works could have been easily captured; but now, with the North full of spies, any attempt to take them by force would have called out all the available strength of South Carolina, assisted by volunteers from other States. On the 10th, it was everywhere published that the Administration intended to withdraw us; but no admission of the kind could be obtained from Mr. Lincoln.[2]

Learning that we had nothing but pork and hard biscuit to eat, Mr. Haight, a wealthy gentleman of New York, sent us several boxes of delicacies. The governor, under the impression we were soon to be withdrawn, allowed them to come over. They were fully appreciated.

The great tobacconist, John Anderson, of New York, also sent a large supply of the best quality of tobacco, having learned that the men felt the loss of their smoking more than anything else.

By this time the South Carolina treasury was in a state of collapse. A loan for six hundred and seventy-five thousand dollars was freely advertised, but no one desired to invest. The city trade, however, began to be quite brisk again, from the immense influx of sympathizing strangers that poured into the city to see the preparations for war. Goods, too, began to come in from all quarters, and there was a gleam of prosperity.

On the 20th, G.W. Lay, one of General Scott's aids, who had resigned on the 2nd of the month, came down to offer his services to Governor Pickens. He must have had in his possession much valuable military and diplomatic information, to which his late confidential position had given him access.

---

2. About this time, my wife, who was in Washington, was very much surprised at receiving a call from the President. He came quietly to request her to show him my letters from Fort Sumter, so that he might form a better opinion as to the condition of affairs there, more particularly in regard to our resources.

On the 21st, another messenger, Captain G.V. Fox, United States Navy, came over to see us. Captain Hartstein, who was an ex-officer of our navy, and an old friend of Fox's, was sent with him, to be within ear-shot, and see that he did no harm to the Confederacy. Fox had an excellent plan of his own in reference to us, and came to reconnoitre, and ascertain whether it was practicable to carry it out; for the President had now fully determined not to withdraw us, or surrender Fort Sumter without an effort to hold and re-enforce it. Indeed, there came up an indignant roar from the great North-west, and many parts of the North, that could not be disregarded with impunity. To have done so would almost have created a revolution.

I was struck by one modest question which Hartstein put to me on this occasion. He asked if I thought Anderson would object to his anchoring the iron-plated floating-battery within a hundred yards of our main gates. Upon my expressing my surprise at such an audacious proposal, he replied, "Anderson has allowed these batteries to be built around him, and has permitted so many things to be done, that I don't see why he should not go a step farther and allow this."

On the 22nd, we learned that Beauregard had assumed command of the forces opposite to us. As he had just left our army, where he had been highly trusted and honoured, it is said he displayed a good deal of feeling at finding himself opposed to the flag under which he had served so long. He expressed much sympathy for his old friend, Anderson, who, he stated, was merely fulfilling his duty as a soldier in fighting for his own Government, and asserted that he would not attack us, even if we withdrew all our sentinels, but would force us to surrender by cutting off our supplies.

On the 23rd, we had but two days' regular fuel left, but we had contrived to secure and utilize a number of floating logs as they passed the fort, and these increased the amount on hand to some extent.

Anderson now had no doubt that we would be withdrawn, and the papers all gave out the same idea. Under these circumstances, as we were out of fuel, and had a large number of surplus gun-carriages on hand which we could not possibly use, and which would inevitably fall into the hands of the enemy when we left, I suggested that it would be good policy to use them for fire-wood, especially as many of them were decayed and worthless. He would not, however, consent to this. Perhaps he thought fuel at six hundred dollars a cord was rather dear. The result was that they were finally all turned over to the Confederacy, with the other public property on hand.

On the 25th, Colonel Ward C. Lamon, the former law-partner of Mr. Lincoln, came over to visit us under charge of Colonel Duryea, of Charleston. It was given out that he was sent as an agent of the General Government to see Governor Pickens in relation to post-office matters; but in reality he came to confer with Anderson, and ascertain the amount of provisions on hand. He took with him the important information that our food would be out by the middle of April.

On the 28th, Beauregard sent a message of some kind to Anderson. I do not know its purport. The latter stated to us that he expected decisive orders from Washington on the 29th, but none came.

The 1st of April arrived, and as the heavy work of mounting guns, etc., was completed, our commander thought it would be a good idea to send off the hired labourers, and he intrusted Captain Foster to ask permission of the rebel authorities to allow them to land. The request was granted, and all left with the exception of a few, who desired to remain with us and share our fortunes. Among them was Mr. William O. Lyman, the principal overseer of the masons, a brave and reliable man.

On the 3rd of April, another affair occurred similar to that of the *Star of the West*. The schooner *R.H. Shannon*, of Boston, under Captain Mounts, *en route* for Savannah with a cargo of ice, sailed into the harbour of Charleston on account of a fog. As the captain did not read the papers, he did not know that anything unusual was going on. A battery on Morris Island fired a shot across the bow of his vessel to bring her to. Very much astonished at this proceeding, he ran up the Stars and Stripes to show that he was all right. This was regarded as a direct defiance,

80

and a heavy cannonade was at once opened on the vessel. Very much puzzled to account for this hostility, he lowered his flag, and the firing ceased. A boat's crew now put off from the shore to ascertain his character and purpose in entering the harbour. While this was going on, we were formed at our guns, in readiness to fire, but were not allowed to do so, although there was every probability that the vessel would be sunk before our eyes.

It is true we could not have reached the particular battery that was doing the mischief; but the other works of the enemy were all under our guns, and, not expecting immediate action, were in a measure unprepared. Anderson, however, contented himself with sending Seymour and Snyder over in a boat with a white flag to ask for an explanation, with the usual result: Lieutenant Talbot and Lieutenant Snyder were then sent over to have an interview with the governor in relation to this matter. This being far from satisfactory, Lieutenant Snyder returned to Fort Sumter, and Lieutenant Talbot kept on his way to Washington with dispatches.

Although this affair attracted very little attention or comment at the North, I was convinced, from the major's depression of spirits, that it acted a great deal upon his mind. He evidently feared it might be considered as a betrayal of his trust, and he was very sensitive to everything that affected his honour.

I have already stated the reasons for his inaction. In amplifying his instructions not to provoke a collision into instructions not to fight at all, I have no doubt he thought he was rendering a real service to the country. He knew the first shot fired by us would light the flames of a civil war that would convulse the world, and tried to put off the evil day as long as possible. Yet a better analysis of the situation might have taught him that the contest had already commenced, and could no longer be avoided. The leaders of the South at this period would hardly have been satisfied with the most abject submission of the antislavery party to all their behests.

In fact, every concession made to their wishes seemed to them to be dictated by the weakness of the Government, and its fears of internal dissensions and civil war in all the great cities of the North. They needed blood and the prestige of a victory to rouse the enthusiasm of their followers, and cement the rising Confederacy. They wanted a new and powerful slave empire, extending to the Isthmus of Panama, and for this a direct issue must be made with the free States. In vain did a member of Congress, who afterward became a distinguished Union general, offer in Richmond to raise an army of twenty thousand men in the North to fight the abolitionists, if the South would consent to remain in the Union. Even this was not deemed sufficient or satisfactory. Slavery had so long dominated everything with a rod of iron, that its votaries deemed it was born to universal dominion. All the pathways to political power, all the avenues of promotion in the army and navy, lay in that direction. General Scott was accustomed to say that "with Virginia officers and Yankee troops he could conquer the world," and this implied that slave-holders, in his opinion, were the only men fitted to command.

Washington was too full of spies for the rebel leaders to remain in ignorance of Lincoln's intention to re-enforce us. On the 6th of April, Beauregard restricted our marketing to two days in the week. On the 7th, it was wholly cut off, and we noticed gangs of negroes hard at work strengthening the defences on Morris Island. Everything betokened that the conflict would soon take place. Anderson was greatly troubled at the failure of all his plans to keep the place. The rebels knew, and perhaps he knew, that on the 6th and 7th of April a number of naval vessels had left New York and Norfolk under sealed orders.

Their destination could hardly be doubted. Lieutenant Talbot reached Washington on the 6th, but was immediately sent back with a message from the President to Governor Pickens, notifying the latter that the Government intended to provision Fort Sumter at all hazards. This formal notice was given by the President, probably because he considered himself bound to do so before putting an end to the semi-pacific code which had governed Anderson's intercourse with the forces around him ever since the departure of Hall and Hayne for Washington.

Talbot delivered his message on the 8th. Beauregard immediately telegraphed the information to the rebel Secretary of War, at Montgomery, Alabama, and received orders on the 10th to open fire at once upon Fort Sumter.

I think it was on the 9th that the official letter came, notifying Anderson that a naval expedition had been sent to our relief, and that he must co-operate with it to the best of his ability. He communicated this information to us on the 10th, but desired it should be kept secret. The preparations we were obliged to make told the men plainly enough, however, that the fighting was about to commence. The news acted like magic upon them. They had previously been drooping and dejected; but they now sprung to their work with the greatest alacrity, laughing, singing, whistling, and full of glee. They were overjoyed to learn that their long imprisonment in the fort would soon be at an end. They had felt themselves humiliated by the open supervision which South Carolina exercised over us, and our tame submission to it. It was very galling to them to see the revenue-cutter, which had been stolen from the United States, anchored within a stone's cast of our walls, to watch our movements and overhaul everything coming to or going from the fort, including our mail-boat.

On the 10th, Beauregard announced his personal staff to consist of Colonels Wigfall, Chestnut, Means, M'Gowan, Manning, and Boyleston.

On the same day, a house directly opposite to us in Moultrieville, at the nearest point, was suddenly removed, disclosing a formidable masked battery, which effectually enfiladed two rows of our upper tier of guns in barbette, and took a third tier in reverse. It was a sad surprise to us, for we had our heaviest metal there. I set to work immediately to construct sand-bag traverses; but it was difficult to make much progress, as we had no bags, and were obliged to tear up sheets for the purpose, and have the pieces sewed together. This labour, however, was entirely thrown away, for Anderson ordered us to abandon all the guns on the parapet. This, of course, was much less dangerous for the men, but it deprived us of the most powerful and effective part of our armament.

About 3 p.m. of the same day, a boat came over with Colonel James Chestnut, Ex-United States Senator, and Captain Stephen D. Lee, both aids of Beauregard. They bore a demand for the surrender of the fort. Anderson politely declined to accede to this request, but stated in conversation he would soon be starved out. This gratuitous information ought never to have been given to the enemy, in view of the fact that a naval expedition was on its way to us.

It was at once supposed that Anderson desired to surrender without fighting; and about 11 p.m. another boat came over, containing Colonel Chestnut, Colonel Pryor, and Captain Lee, to inquire upon what day he would be willing to evacuate the work in case he was not attacked. The answer was, on the 15th at noon, provided he did not receive fresh instructions, or was not relieved before that time. As we had pork enough on hand to last for two weeks longer, there was no necessity for fixing so early a day. It left too little margin for naval operations, as, in all probability, the vessels, in case of any accident or detention, would arrive too late to be of service. This proved to be the case.

The enemy's batteries on Sullivan's Island were so placed as to fire directly into the officers' quarters at Fort Sumter; and as our rooms would necessarily become untenable, we vacated them, and chose points that were more secure. I moved my bed into a magazine which was directly opposite to Cummings Point, and which was nearly empty. As I was sensible that the next three days would call for great physical exertion and constant wakefulness, I endeavoured to get all the sleep I could on the night of the 11th.

About 4 a.m. on the 12th, I was awakened by someone groping about my room in the dark and calling out my name. It proved to be Anderson, who came to announce to me that he had just received a dispatch from Beauregard, dated 3.20 a.m., to the effect that he should open fire upon us in an hour. Finding it was determined not to return the fire until after breakfast, I remained in bed. As we had no lights, we could in fact do nothing before that time, except to wander around in the darkness, and fire without an accurate view of the enemy's works.

CHAPTER 10

The Bombardment

As soon as the outline of our fort could be distinguished, the enemy carried out their programme. It had been arranged, as a special compliment to the venerable Edmund Ruffin, who might almost be called the father of secession, that he should fire the first shot against us, from the Stevens battery on Cummings Point, and I think in all the histories it is stated that he did so; but it is attested by Dr. Crawford and others who were on the parapet at the time, that the first shot really came from the mortar battery at Fort Johnson.[1] Almost immediately afterward a ball from Cummings Point lodged in the magazine wall, and by the sound seemed to bury itself in the masonry about a foot from my head, in very unpleasant proximity to my right ear.

This is the one that probably came with Mr. Ruffin's compliments. In a moment the firing burst forth in one continuous roar, and large patches of both the exterior and interior masonry began to crumble and fall in all directions. The place where I was had been used for the manufacture of cartridges, and there was still a good deal of powder there, some packed and some loose. A shell soon struck near the ventilator, and a puff of dense smoke entered the room, giving me a strong impression that there would be an immediate explosion. Fortunately, no sparks had penetrated inside.

Nineteen batteries were now hammering at us, and the balls and shells from the ten-inch *columbiads*, accompanied by shells

---

1. I have since learned that the shell from Fort Johnson was not a hostile shot, but was simply intended as a signal for the firing to commence.

from the thirteen-inch mortars which constantly bombarded us, made us feel as if the war had commenced in earnest.

When it was broad daylight, I went down to breakfast. I found the officers already assembled at one of the long tables in the mess-hall. Our party were calm, and even somewhat merry. We had retained one coloured man to wait on us. He was a spruce-looking mulatto from Charleston, very active and efficient on ordinary occasions, but now completely demoralized by the thunder of the guns and crashing of the shot around us. He leaned back against the wall, almost white with fear, his eyes closed, and his whole expression one of perfect despair.[2] Our meal was not very sumptuous. It consisted of pork and water, but Dr. Crawford triumphantly brought forth a little farina, which he had found in a corner of the hospital.

When this frugal repast was over, my company was told off in three details for firing purposes, to be relieved afterward by Seymour's company. As I was the ranking officer, I took the first detachment, and marched them to the casemates, which looked out upon the powerful iron-clad battery of Cummings Point.

In aiming the first gun fired against the rebellion I had no feeling of self-reproach, for I fully believed that the contest was inevitable, and was not of our seeking. The United States was called upon not only to defend its sovereignty, but its right to exist as a nation. The only alternative was to submit to a powerful oligarchy who were determined to make freedom forever subordinate to slavery. To me it was simply a contest, politically speaking, as to whether virtue or vice should rule.

My first shot bounded off from the sloping roof of the battery opposite without producing any apparent effect. It seemed useless to attempt to silence the guns there; for our metal was not heavy enough to batter the work down, and every ball glanced harmlessly off, except one, which appeared to enter an embrasure and twist the iron shutter, so as to stop the firing of

---

2. In this he was an exception to most negroes. Those I have seen in the coloured regiments in Texas have shown themselves to be among the best and most reliable men in the service for operations against the Indians. It was a line of negroes that charged over the torpedoes at Mobile

that particular gun.

I observed that a group of the enemy had ventured out from their intrenchments to watch the effect of their fire, but I sent them flying back to their shelter by the aid of a forty-two-pounder ball, which appeared to strike right in among them.

Assistant-surgeon Crawford, having no sick in hospital, volunteered to take command of one of the detachments. He and Lieutenant Davis were detailed at the same time with me; and I soon heard their guns on the opposite side of the fort, echoing my own. They attacked Fort Moultrie with great vigour.

Our firing now became regular, and was answered from the rebel guns which encircled us on the four sides of the pentagon upon which the fort was built. The other side faced the open sea. Showers of balls from ten-inch *columbiads* and forty-two-pounders, and shells from thirteen-inch mortars poured into the fort in one incessant stream, causing great flakes of masonry to fall in all directions. When the immense mortar shells, after sailing high in the air, came down in a vertical direction, and buried themselves in the parade-ground, their explosion shook the fort like an earthquake.[3]

Our own guns were very defective, as they had no breech-sights. In place of these, Seymour and myself were obliged to devise notched sticks, which answered the purpose, but were necessarily very imperfect.

Our fort had been built with reference to the penetration of shot when the old system of smooth-bore guns prevailed. The balls from a new Blakely gun on Cummings Point, however, had force enough to go entirely through the wall which sheltered us, and some of the fragments of brick which were knocked out wounded several of my detachment. None were seriously hurt

3. The troops and defences on Morris Island were commanded by Brigadier-general James W. Simons. The artillery was under the command of Colonel Wilmot G. De Saussure, of the South Carolina Artillery Battalion.
Sullivan's Island was commanded by Brigadier-general John Dunovant, formerly an officer of the United States Army. His second in command was Lieutenant-colonel Roswell S. Ripley, of the South Carolina Artillery Battalion, formerly of our army. Major N.G. Evans, assistant adjutant-general, commanded on James Island.
The battery at Mount Pleasant was under the command of Captain Robert Martin, of the South Carolina Infantry.

except Sergeant Thomas Kirnan, of my company. His contusions were severe, but did not keep him out of the fight.

After three hours' firing, my men became exhausted, and Captain Seymour came, with a fresh detachment, to relieve us. He has a great deal of humour in his composition, and said, jocosely, "Doubleday, what in the world is the matter here, and what is all this uproar about?"

I replied, "There is a trifling difference of opinion between us and our neighbours opposite, and we are trying to settle it."

"Very well," he said; "do you wish me to take a hand?"

I said, "Yes, I would like to have you go in."

"All right," he said. "What is your elevation, and range?"

I replied, "Five degrees, and twelve hundred yards."

"Well," he said, "here goes!" And he went to work with a will.

Part of the fleet was visible outside the bar about half-past ten a.m. It exchanged salutes with us, but did not attempt to enter the harbour, or take part in the battle. In fact, it would have had considerable difficulty in finding the channel, as the marks and buoys had all been taken up. It was composed originally of the frigates *Pawnee*, under Commodore Rowan; the *Pocahontas*, under Captain Gillis; the *Powhatan*, under Captain Mercer; the steam transport *Baltic*, under Captain Fletcher; and, I believe, the steam-tugs *Yankee, Uncle Ben*, and another, which was not permitted to leave New York. The soldiers on board consisted of two hundred and fifty recruits from Governor's Island, under command of First Lieutenants E.M.K. Hudson, of the Fourth, and Robert O. Tyler, of the Third Artillery, and Second Lieutenant A.I. Thomas, of the First Infantry.

This expedition was designed by Captain Fox, in consultation with G.W. Blunt, William H. Aspinwall, Russel Sturges, and others. After the event much obloquy was thrown upon the navy because it did not come in and engage the numerous batteries and forts, and open for itself a way to Charleston; but this course would probably have resulted in the sinking of every vessel.

As far back as December I had written to New York that it was very difficult for a gun on shore to hit a small boat dancing on the waves in the daytime, and at night it is almost impossible. I suggested, therefore, that we might be re-enforced and provisioned by means of a number of small boats, supplied from several naval vessels as a base of operations. The same idea had occurred to Captain Fox; and on the present occasion he had brought thirty launches to be used for this purpose. They were to be manned by three hundred sailors, and in case they were assailed, the fleet was to protect them as far as possible by its guns.

Unfortunately, the different vessels did not reach the rendezvous together. The *Pawnee* and *Pocahontas* arrived on the 12th, but lost a great deal of time in waiting for the *Powhatan*, which contained the launches and other arrangements, without which a boat expedition could not be organized. The *Powhatan* never appeared, having been unexpectedly detached, by order of the President, at the solicitation of Secretary Seward, and without consultation with the Navy Department. I think the *Baltic* was detained by running upon Rattlesnake Shoal. The steam-tug *Uncle Ben* was driven into Wilmington by a storm, and the *Yankee* did not make its appearance until the 15th. The expedition was thus an utter failure.

Nevertheless, a passing schooner was purchased and loaded up with provisions and soldiers, and an attempt would have been made to run in on the night of the 13th, but by that time it was too late. The fort had surrendered.

Having explained this matter, we will now resume the narrative of our operations. For the next three hours a vigorous fire was kept up on both sides. A great many shots were aimed at our flag-staff, but nearly all of them passed above the fort and struck in the water beyond. I think we succeeded in silencing several guns in Fort Moultrie, and one or more in the Stevens battery.

When Seymour's three hours were up, I relieved him, and continued the firing. As our balls bounded off the sloping iron rails like peas upon a trencher, utterly failing to make any impression, and as the shot from the Blakely gun came clear through our walls, Anderson directed that the men should cease firing at that particular place. I regretted very much that the upper tier of guns had been abandoned, as they were all loaded and pointed, and were of very heavy calibre. A wild Irish soldier, however, named John Carmody, slipped up on the parapet, and, without orders, fired the pieces there, one after another, on his own account. One of the ten-inch balls so aimed made quite an impression on the Cummings Point battery; and if the fire could have been kept up, it might possibly have knocked the iron-work to pieces.

After my detachment had abandoned the casemate opposite the Blakely gun, to my great astonishment the battery I had left recommenced firing. I could not imagine who could have taken our places. It seems that a group of the Baltimore workmen had been watching our motions, and had thus learned the duties of a cannoneer. In spite of their previous determination not to take part in the fight, they could not resist the fun of trying their hand at one of the guns. It was already accurately pointed, and the ball struck the mark in the centre. The men attributed it to their own skill, and when I entered they were fairly in convulsions of laughter. One of them, in answer to my question, gasped out, "I hit it square in the middle." After this first attempt, each of them was desirous of trying his skill at aiming. The result was, that we soon had them organized into a firing-party.

Finding one of my chests had been left in the officers' quarters, and that it would probably be knocked to pieces by the shells, I asked the mulatto, who still sat back against the wall, apparently asleep, to bear a hand and help me bring it out. He opened his eyes, shook his head dolefully, and said, "De major, he say, I muss not expose myself."

If I mistake not, Roswell S. Ripley, formerly a brevet major in our army, fired the second or third shot to bring down the flag under which he had served for so many years. Ripley was born in Ohio, appointed from New York, and educated at the Military Academy. He had, therefore, even on the Southern theory of State rights, no necessary affiliation with the South. In fact, they always despised a man who joined them to fight against his own State. In one instance, Jeff Davis himself had to use all his influence to induce the Southern troops to obey one of these

Northern generals.

Ripley had previously been engaged as an agent for Sharpe's Arms Company in Europe; and, having been unsuccessful there, came to Charleston, with the hope of repairing his shattered fortunes by selling guns to South Carolina. Through the influence of Colonel Huger, of our Ordnance Department, who was in the city at the time, Ripley failed in this, and, being entirely out of employment, accepted a commission from the Confederacy to fight against his old comrades. Being a man of talent, and a skilful artillerist, he did us a great deal of harm. Like all Northern converts, he thought it necessary to be overzealous in his new position, to do away with the suspicions excited by his birth and education. I was told at the time that for this purpose he took pains to denounce me as an Abolitionist, and to recommend that I be hanged by the populace as soon as caught.

The firing continued all day, without any special incident of importance, and without our making much impression on the enemy's works. They had a great advantage over us, as their fire was concentrated on the fort, which was in the centre of the circle, while ours was diffused over the circumference. Their missiles were exceedingly destructive to the upper exposed portion of the work, but no essential injury was done to the lower casemates which sheltered us.

Some of these shells, however, set the officers' quarters on fire three times; but the flames were promptly extinguished once or twice through the exertions of Peter Hart, whose activity and gallantry were very conspicuous.

The night was an anxious one for us, for we thought it probable that the launches, filled with armed men from the fleet, might take advantage of the darkness to come in with provisions and supplies. Then, too, it was possible that the enemy might attempt a night attack. We were on the alert, therefore, with men stationed at all the embrasures; but nothing unusual occurred. The batteries fired upon us at stated intervals all night long. We did not return the fire, having no ammunition to waste.

On the morning of the 13th, we took our breakfast—or, rather, our pork and water—at the usual hour, and marched the men to the guns when the meal was over.

From 4 to 6.30 a.m. the enemy's fire was very spirited. From 7 to 8 a.m. a rainstorm came on, and there was a lull in the cannonading. About 8 a.m. the officers' quarters were ignited by one of Ripley's incendiary shells, or by shot heated in the furnaces at Fort Moultrie. The fire was put out; but at 10 a.m. a mortar shell passed through the roof, and lodged in the flooring of the second story, where it burst, and started the flames afresh. This, too, was extinguished; but the hot shot soon followed each other so rapidly that it was impossible for us to contend with them any longer.

It became evident that the entire block, being built with wooden partitions, floors, and roofing, must be consumed, and that the magazine, containing three hundred barrels of powder, would be endangered; for, even after closing the metallic door, sparks might penetrate through the ventilator. The floor was covered with loose powder, where a detail of men had been at work manufacturing cartridge-bags out of old shirts, woollen blankets, etc.

While the officers exerted themselves with axes to tear down and cut away all the wood-work in the vicinity, the soldiers were rolling barrels of powder out to more sheltered spots, and were covering them with wet blankets. The labour was accelerated by the shells which were bursting around us; for Ripley had re-doubled his activity at the first signs of a conflagration. We only succeeded in getting out some ninety-six barrels of powder, and then we were obliged to close the massive copper door, and await the result. A shot soon after passed through the intervening shield, struck the door, and bent the lock in such a way that it could not be opened again. We were thus cut off from our supply of ammunition, but still had some piled up in the vicinity of the guns. Anderson officially reported only four barrels and three cartridges as on hand when we left.

By 11 a.m. the conflagration was terrible and disastrous. One-fifth of the fort was on fire, and the wind drove the smoke in dense masses into the angle where we had all taken refuge. It seemed impossible to escape suffocation. Some lay down close to the ground, with handkerchiefs over their mouths, and others posted themselves near the embrasures, where the smoke was somewhat lessened by the draught of air. Every one suffered severely. I crawled out of one of these openings, and sat on the outer edge; but Ripley made it lively for me there with his case-shot, which spattered all around. Had not a slight change of wind taken place, the result might have been fatal to most of us.

Our firing having ceased, and the enemy being very jubilant, I thought it would be as well to show them that we were not all dead yet, and ordered the gunners to fire a few rounds more. I heard afterward that the enemy loudly cheered Anderson for his persistency under such adverse circumstances.

The scene at this time was really terrific. The roaring and crackling of the flames, the dense masses of whirling smoke, the bursting of the enemy's shells, and our own which were exploding in the burning rooms, the crashing of the shot, and the sound of masonry falling in every direction, made the fort a pandemonium.

When at last nothing was left of the building but the blackened walls and smouldering embers, it became painfully evident that an immense amount of damage had been done. There was a tower at each angle of the fort. One of these, containing great quantities of shells, upon which we had relied, was almost completely shattered by successive explosions. The massive wooden gates, studded with iron nails, were burned, and the wall built behind them was now a mere heap of *débris*, so that the main entrance was wide open for an assaulting party. The sally-ports were in a similar condition, and the numerous windows on the gorge side, which had been planked up, had now become all open entrances.

About 12.48 p.m. the end of the flag-staff was shot down, and the flag fell.[4] It had been previously hanging by one halliard, the other having been cut by a piece of shell. The exultation of the enemy, however, was short-lived. Peter Hart found a spar in the fort, which answered very well as a temporary flag-staff. He

---

4. It is claimed that this shot was fired by Lieutenant W.C. Preston, of South Carolina.

nailed the flag to this, and raised it triumphantly by nailing and tying the pole firmly to a pile of gun-carriages on the parapet. This was gallantly done, without undue haste, under Seymour's supervision, although the enemy concentrated all their fire upon the spot to prevent Hart from carrying out his intention. From the beginning, the rebel gunners had been very ambitious to shoot the flag down, and had wasted an immense number of shots in the attempt.

While the battle was going on, a correspondent of the *New York Tribune*, who was in Charleston, wrote that the populace were calling for my head. Fortunately, I was not there to gratify them. My relations with the gentlemen of Charleston had always been friendly. The enmity of the mob was simply political, and was founded on the belief that I was the only "Black Republican," as they termed it, in the fort.

CHAPTER 11

The Evacuation

There was a large, first-class wooden hotel, near the shore, on Sullivan's Island, called the Moultrie House. It was only kept open during the summer, and was a favourite resort, for planters and others, to enjoy the fresh sea-breeze, and the beautiful drive up the beach at low tide. Since the rebel occupation of Fort Moultrie, this hotel had been used as a *dépôt* and barracks for the troops in the vicinity. Just before the attack was made upon us, the Palmetto flag, which had waved over the building, was taken down; but I noticed with a spy-glass that there was still quite a number of people, apparently troops, remaining in the house.

I saw no reason why the mere lowering of the flag should prevent us from firing at them. I therefore aimed two forty-two pounder balls at the upper story. The crashing of the shot, which went through the whole length of the building among the clapboards and interior partitions, must have been something fearful to those who were within. They came rushing out in furious haste, and tumbled over each other until they reached the bottom of the front steps, in one writhing, tumultuous mass.

When we left Fort Sumter, a South Carolina officer, who seemed to feel aggrieved in relation to this matter, asked me why we fired at that building. Not caring to enter into a discussion at that time, I evaded it by telling him the true reason was, that the landlord had given me a wretched room there one night, and this being the only opportunity that had occurred to get even with him, I was unable to resist it. He laughed heartily, and said, "I understand it all now. You were perfectly right, sir, and I justify the act."

About 2 p.m., Senator Wigfall, in company with W. Gourdin Young, of Charleston, unexpectedly made his appearance at one of the embrasures, having crossed over from Morris Island in a small boat, rowed by negroes. He had seen the flag come down, and supposed that we had surrendered in consequence of the burning of the quarters. This visit was sanctioned by the commander of Morris Island, Brigadier-general James W. Simons. An artillery-man, serving his gun, was very much astonished to see a man's face at the entrance, and asked him what he was doing there. Wigfall replied that he wished to see Major Anderson.

The man, however, refused to allow him to enter until he had surrendered himself as a prisoner, and given up his sword. This done, another artillery-man was sent to bring an officer. Lieutenant Davis came almost immediately, but it took some time to find Anderson, who was out examining the condition of the main gates. I was not present during this scene, or at the interview that ensued, as I was engaged in trying to save some shells in the upper story from the effects of the fire. Wigfall, in Beauregard's name, offered Anderson his own terms, which were, the evacuation of the fort, with permission to salute our flag, and to march out with the honours of war, with our arms and private baggage, leaving all other war material behind. As soon as this matter was arranged, Wigfall returned to Cummings Point.

In the meantime, Beauregard having noticed the white flag, sent a boat containing Colonel James Chestnut, and Captain Lee, Colonel Roger A. Pryor, and Colonel William Porcher Miles, to ascertain the meaning of the signal. A second boat soon followed, containing Major D.K. Jones, who was Beauregard's adjutant-general, Ex-Governor J.L. Manning, and Colonel Charles Alston.

Miles and Pryor were exceedingly astonished when they heard that Wigfall had been carrying on negotiations in Beauregard's name, and stated that, to their certain knowledge, he had had no communication with Beauregard. They spoke of the matter with great delicacy, for Wigfall was a parlous man, and quick to settle disputed points with the pistol. Anderson replied with spirit that, under the circumstances, he would run up his flag again, and resume the firing. They begged him, however, not to take action until they had had an opportunity to lay the whole subject before General Beauregard; and Anderson agreed to wait a reasonable time for that purpose.

The boat then returned to the city. In due time another boat arrived, containing Colonels Chestnut and Chisholm, and Captain Stephen D. Lee, all aids of Beauregard. They came to notify Major Anderson that the latter was willing to treat with him on the basis proposed. Colonel Charles Alston soon came over with Major Jones (who was chief-of-staff to Beauregard, and adjutant-general of the Provisional Army), to settle the details of the evacuation. There was some difficulty about permitting us to salute our flag; but that, too, was finally conceded. In case we held out for another day, the rebels had made arrangements to storm the fort that night.

During all these operations, our officers and men behaved with great gallantry. Hall, Snyder, and Meade had never been under fire before, but they proved themselves to be true sons of their Alma Mater at West Point.

The first contest of the war was over, and had ended as a substantial victory for the Secessionists. They had commenced the campaign naked and defenceless; but the General Government had allowed them time to levy an army against us, and we had permitted ourselves to be surrounded with a ring of fire, from which there was no escape. Nor had we employed to the fullest extent all our available means of defence. No attempt had ever been made to use the upper tier of guns, which contained our heaviest metal, and which, from its height, overlooked the enemy's works, and was, therefore, the most efficient part of our armament.

Although the fire of our *columbiads*, under ordinary circumstances, could not quite reach the city, we had arranged one of them to point upward at the maximum angle. As the carriage would not admit of this, the gun was taken off, and made to rest on a bed of masonry. Seymour and myself thought, by loading it with eccentric shells, we could increase the range of the guns so that the balls would reach that part of Charleston which was nearest to us; but we were not allowed to use the gun at all. It seemed to me there was a manifest desire to do as little damage as possible.

About eighteen hundred shot had been fired into Fort Sumter, and the upper story was pretty well knocked to pieces. To walk around the parapet, we had constantly to climb over heaps of *débris*. With all this expenditure of ammunition, we had but one man dangerously wounded. This was John Schweirer, foreman of the Baltimore brick-layers. He was struck by a piece of shell while standing near the open parade-ground. So long as our men fought in the lower casemates, which were shell-proof, the vertical fire could not reach them; and by drilling them to step one side of the embrasure whenever they saw the flash of a gun opposite, they escaped the danger of being struck by any ball which might enter the opening; so that, on the whole, they ran very little risk. Had they used the guns on the parapet, the number of casualties would have been greatly increased, but our missiles would have been much more effective.

When William Porcher Miles was about to enter the boat to return to Charleston, he told our commander that none of the secession soldiers were injured by our fire. Anderson raised his hands and ejaculated, "Thank God for that!" As the object of our fighting was to do as much damage as possible, I could see no propriety in thanking Heaven for the small amount of injury we had inflicted. I have since had reason to suspect, from several circumstances, that the contest was not as bloodless as it was represented to be at the time.

The coxswain of the boat that brought Miles over heard him make the remark that no one was hurt on the rebel side. The man stared at him for a moment in undisguised amazement, and then stepped aside behind an angle of the work, where he could indulge in a hearty fit of laughter. His whole action was that of one who thought his chief had been indulging in romance. Of course Miles believed the assertion, or he would not have made it.

The fact is, Fort Moultrie was all slivered and knocked to

pieces; and as I heard so much in reference to the narrow escapes of officers and soldiers there, I concluded that, if no one was hurt, a miracle must have taken place. The rebel who carried dispatches between Fort Moultrie and Mount Pleasant in a small boat was in a position to know, and he told Peter Hart, some years after the war, that a schooner, to his certain knowledge, came from Charleston during the battle, and took off a number of killed from Fort Moultrie, who were taken to Potter's Field, on Cooper River, and buried there on Saturday, at 4.30 a.m. I had previously seen the same story published as coming from Charleston. A similar statement was made, on his arrival in New York, by the mate of the schooner D.B. Pitts, and it purported to be founded on his own observation.

When we left Fort Sumter for New York, a man of my company, named Fielding, was seriously injured by an explosion, and left behind in the hospital at Charleston. He was frequently visited there by an old comrade, named Galloway, who was one of our discharged soldiers. Galloway laughed at the idea that no one had been injured, and told Fielding that he himself had served in Fort Moultrie during the bombardment, and had seen with his own eyes a number of killed and wounded there. If Galloway's story is true, Ripley may have concealed his losses, as he did not wish to have us appear more successful than he had been.

I believe there were a great many Irish labourers enlisted in Fort Moultrie, and their loss would hardly have excited a remark in aristocratic Charleston. It is said, too, that a list of killed and wounded was posted up on a bulletin-board in the city, and afterward torn down, for fear that it might discourage the troops. On the other hand, the assertion of men holding high official position on the other side, that no one was killed or injured, would seem to leave little room for doubt.

When Beauregard received notice that Anderson was willing to ratify the terms agreed upon, he sent over another boat, containing Colonel Miles, Colonel Pryor, Ex-Governor Manning, Major Jones, and Captain Hartstein, to arrange the details of the evacuation.

Almost a fatal accident occurred to Roger A. Pryor shortly

after his arrival in the fort. He was sitting in the hospital at a table, with a black bottle and a tumbler near his right hand. The place was quite dark, having been built up all around with boxes of sand, to render it shell-proof. Being thirsty, and not noticing what he did, he mechanically picked up the bottle, poured some of the liquid into the glass, and drank it down. It proved to be iodide of potassium, which is quite a poisonous compound.

When I saw him, he was very pale, and leaning on the shoulder of Dr. Crawford, who was taking him out on the grass to apply the stomach-pump. He was soon out of danger. Some of us questioned the doctor's right to interpose in a case of this kind. It was argued that if any rebel leader chose to come over to Fort Sumter and poison himself, the Medical Department had no business to interfere with such a laudable intention. The doctor, however, claimed, with some show of reason, that he himself was held responsible to the United States for the medicine in the hospital, and therefore he could not permit Pryor to carry any of it away.

All of the preliminaries having been duly adjusted, it was decided that the evacuation should take place the next morning. Our arrangements were few and simple, but the rebels made extensive preparations for the event, in order to give it the greatest *éclat*, and gain from it as much prestige as possible. The population of the surrounding country poured into Charleston in vast multitudes, to witness the humiliation of the United States flag. We slept soundly that night for the first time, after all the fatigue and excitement of the two preceding days.

The next morning, Sunday, the 14th, we were up early, packing our baggage in readiness to go on board the transport. The time having arrived, I made preparations, by order of Major Anderson, to fire a national salute to the flag. It was a dangerous thing to attempt, as sparks of fire were floating around everywhere, and there was no safe place to deposit the ammunition.

In that portion of the line commanded by Lieutenant Hall, a pile of cartridges lay under the muzzle of one of the guns. Some fire had probably lodged inside the piece, which the sponging did not extinguish, for, in loading it, it went off prematurely, and blew off the right arm of the gunner, Daniel Hough, who was an excellent soldier. His death was almost instantaneous. He was the first man who lost his life on our side in the war for the Union. The damage did not end here, for some of the fire from the muzzle dropped on the pile of cartridges below, and exploded them all. Several men in the vicinity were blown into the air, and seriously injured. Their names were George Fielding, John Irwin, George Pinchard, and Edwin Galway, and, I think, James Hayes. The first-named being very badly hurt, was left behind, to be cared for by the rebels. He was sent over to Charleston, where he was well treated, finally cured, and forwarded to us without being exchanged.

The salute being over, the Confederate troops marched in to occupy the fort. The Palmetto Guard, Captain Cuthbert's company, detailed by Colonel De Saussure, and Captain Hollinquist's Company B, of the regulars, detailed by Colonel Ripley, constituted the new garrison under Ripley.[1] Anderson directed me to form the men on the parade-ground, assume command, and march them on board the transport. I told him I should prefer to leave the fort with the flag flying, and the drums beating Yankee Doodle, and he authorized me to do so.

As soon as our tattered flag came down, and the silken banner made by the ladies of Charleston was run up, tremendous shouts of applause were heard from the vast multitude of spectators; and all the vessels and steamers, with one accord, made for the fort. Corporal Bringhurst came running to tell me that many of the approaching crowd were shouting my name, and making threatening demonstrations. The disorder, however, was immediately quelled by the appearance of Hartstein, an ex-officer of our navy, who threw out sentinels in all directions, and prevented the mob from landing.

The bay was alive with floating craft of every description, filled with people from all parts of the South, in their holiday attire. As I marched out at the head of our little band of regulars, it must have presented a strange contrast to the numerous forces that had assailed us; some sixty men against six thousand. As we went on board the *Isabel*, with the drums beating the national air, all eyes were fixed upon us amidst the deepest silence. It was an hour of triumph for the originators of secession in South Carolina, and no doubt it seemed to

---

1. Edmund Ruffin entered the fort as a volunteer ensign of the Palmetto Guard; Captain Samuel Ferguson received the keys of Fort Sumter, and raised the Confederate flag over the ramparts; Lieutenant-colonel F.J. Moses raised the State flag. Moses has since figured as the Republican governor of South Carolina.

them the culmination of all their hopes; but could they have seen into the future with the eye of prophecy, their joy might have been turned into mourning.

Who among them could have conceived that the Charleston they deemed so invincible, which they boasted would never be polluted by the footsteps of a Yankee invader until every son of the soil had shed the last drop of his blood in her defence—who could have imagined that this proud metropolis, after much privation and long-suffering from fire and bombardment, would finally surrender, without bloodshed, to a negro regiment, under a Massachusetts flag—the two most abhorred elements of the strife to the proud people of South Carolina? Who could have imagined that the race they had so despised was destined to govern them in the future, in the dense ignorance which the South itself had created, by prohibiting the education of the blacks?

My story is nearly done. We soon reached the *Baltic*, and were received with great sympathy and feeling by the army and navy officers present. Among the latter was Captain Fox, who afterward became the Assistant Secretary of the Navy.

It is worthy of remark that, after we had left the harbour, Bishop Lynch, of Charleston, threw the Catholic influence in favour of the Secessionists by celebrating the Southern victory by a grand *Te Deum*.

We arrived in New York on the 19th, and were received with unbounded enthusiasm. All the passing steamers saluted us with their steam-whistles and bells, and cheer after cheer went up from the ferry-boats and vessels in the harbour. We did not attempt to land, but came to anchor in the stream, between Governor's Island and the Battery. Several distinguished citizens at once came on board, and Major Anderson was immediately carried off to dine with Mr. Lloyd Aspinwall. As somebody had to remain with the troops and attend to their wants, I accompanied them to Fort Hamilton, where we soon found ourselves in comfortable quarters. Nearly all of the officers obtained a furlough immediately; but I remained in command of the fort during the temporary absence of Major Anderson, who was soon after permanently detached from us.

Our captivity had deeply touched the hearts of the people, and every day the number of visitors almost amounted to an ovation. The principal city papers, the *Tribune, Times, Herald*, and *Evening Post*, gave us a hearty welcome. For a long time the enthusiasm in New York remained undiminished. It was impossible for us to venture into the main streets without being ridden on the shoulders of men, and torn to pieces by hand-shaking. Shortly after our arrival, Henry Ward Beecher came down to the fort to meet us, and made a ringing speech, full of fire and patriotism. It seemed as if every one of note called to express his devotion to the cause of the Union, and his sympathy with us, who had been its humble representatives amidst the perils of the first conflict of the war.

As I have stated, of the officers who were engaged in the operations herein narrated, but four now survive.

George W. Snyder was the first to leave us. He was present in the battle of Bull Run, attained the brevet of captain, and died in Washington, District of Columbia, on the 17th of November, 1861.

Theodore Talbot became assistant-adjutant-general, with the rank of major, and died on the 22nd of April, 1862, also in Washington.

Richard K. Meade was induced, by the pressure of social and family ties, to resign his commission in our army. He became a rebel officer, and died at Petersburg, Virginia, in July, 1862.

Norman J. Hall became colonel of the Seventh Michigan Volunteers, and received three brevets in the regular army, the last being for gallant and distinguished services at Gettysburg. He died on the 26th of May, 1867, at Brooklyn, New York.

John L. Gardner received the brevet of brigadier-general, and was retired at the commencement of the war. He died at Wilmington, Delaware, on the 19th of February, 1869.

Robert Anderson was made a brigadier-general, and afterward a brevet major-general, for his services at Fort Sumter. He served about six months as Commander of the Department of Kentucky and of the Cumberland, and was then obliged to leave the field in consequence of ill health. He was retired from active service on the 27th of October, 1863, and died at Nice, in France, on the 26th day of October, 1871.

Lastly, John G. Foster, after a brilliant career as commander of a department and army corps, died at Nashua, New Hampshire, September 2nd, 1874.

Each of us who survive became major-general during the rebellion, and each now holds the same grade by brevet in the regular army.

Mr. Edward Moale, the citizen who remained with us, did excellent service in the war. At present he is a brevet lieutenant-colonel in the regular army.

This statement of events was completed at New York, April 14th, 1875, on the fourteenth anniversary of the evacuation of Fort Sumter.

Appendix

List of Officers and Enlisted Men present at the Bombardment of Fort Sumter, April 12th and 13th, 1861.

Commissioned Officers

Major Robert Anderson, First United States Artillery. Captain Abner Doubleday, First United States Artillery. Captain Truman Seymour, First United States Artillery. First Lieutenant Jefferson C. Davis, First United States Artillery. Second Lieutenant Norman J. Hall, First United States Artillery. Captain J.G. Foster, United States Engineers. Lieutenant G.W. Snyder, United States Engineers. Lieutenant R.K. Meade, United States Engineers. Assistant Surgeon S.W. Crawford, United States Army.

Enlisted Men.

Ordnance-sergeant James Kearney, United States Army. Quartermaster-sergeant William H. Hammer, First United States Artillery.

Regimental Band, First Artillery.

Sergeant James E. Galway. Corporal Andrew Smith. Private Andrew Murphy. Private Fedeschi Onoratti. Private Peter Rice. Private Henry Schmidt. Private John Urquhart. Private Andrew Wickstrom.

Company E, First Artillery.

First Sergeant Eugene Scheibner. Sergeant Thomas Kirnan. Sergeant William A. Harn. Sergeant James Chester. Corporal Owen M'Guire. Corporal Francis J. Oakes. Corporal Charles Bringhurst. Corporal Henry Ellerbrook. Musician Charles Hall. Private Philip Anderman. Private John Emil Noack. Private Cornelius Baker. Private Thomas Carroll. Private Patrick Clancy. Private John Davis. Private James Digdam. Private George Fielding. Private Edward Gallway. Private James Gibbons. Private James Hays. Private Daniel Hough. Private John Irwin. Private James M'Donald. Private Samuel Miller.

Private John Newport. Private George Pinchard. Private Frank Rivers. Private Lewis Schroeder. Private Carl A. Sellman. Private John Thompson. Private Charles H. Tozer. Private William Witzman.

COMPANY H, FIRST ARTILLERY.

First Sergeant John Renehan. Sergeant James M'Mahon. Sergeant John Carmody. Sergeant John Otto. Corporal Christopher Costolan. Musician Robert Foster. Artificer Henry Strandt. Private Edward Brady. Private Barney Cain. Private John Doran. Private Dennis Johnson. Private John Kehoe. Private John Klein. Private John Lanagan. Private Frederick Lintner. Private John Magill. Private John Laroche. Private Frederick Meier. Private James Moore. Private William Morter. Private Patrick Neilan. Private John Nixon. Private Michael O'Donald. Private Robert Roe. Private William Walker. Private Joseph Wall. Private Edmond Walsh. Private Henry R. Walter. Private Herman Will. Private Thomas Wishnowski. Private Casper Wutterpel.

LIST OF MECHANICS AND EMPLOYÉS PRESENT IN FORT SUMTER DURING THE BOMBARDMENT, APRIL 12TH AND 13TH, 1861.

EMPLOYÉS OF THE ENGINEER DEPARTMENT.

George Coons, mason. John Schweirer, mason. John Buckley, smith. John Lindsay, carpenter. John Saxton, rigger. James Tweedle, smith. Wm. O. Lyman, overseer.

LABOURERS.

Michael Berne. John Burns. John Branley. Peter Caine. Patrick Conner. Michael Cummins. William Dorsey. Edward Davis. Patrick Donahoe. Peter Donley. William Eagen. Andrew Felton. Michael Goff. James Howlett. Patrick Heeney. Andrew Lindsey. Dennis Magrath. John M'Carty. James M'Mahon. Michael Meechins. Thomas Murphy. Thomas Myers. William Powers. Edward Quinn. Patrick Quinn. Martin Rafferty. John Riley. Michael Ryan. Jeremiah Ryan. James Ryan. James Shea.

COOKS.

Samuel Abraze. Patrick Walsh.

The following is taken from a South Carolina official document, but it seems somewhat defective in detail:

LIST OF CONFEDERATE BATTERIES CONSTRUCTED WITH A VIEW TO THE REDUCTION OF FORT SUMTER.

ON MORRIS ISLAND.

Brigadier-general James W. Simons, commanding; Colonel Wilmot G. De Saussure, commanding Artillery Battalion. Lieutenant J. R. Macbeth, Captain J. Jones, and Lieutenant F.L. Childs, acting as aids to Colonel De Saussure.

STEVENS BATTERY. (FIRED 1200 SHOTS.)

Three Eight-inch columbiads.

Garrisoned by the Palmetto Guard, Captain George B. Cuthbert commanding; Lieutenant G.L. Buist. The ammunition was served out by Mr. Philips and Mr. Campbell. One gun was disabled on Friday.

CUMMINGS POINT BATTERY.

Two forty-two-pounders, three ten-inch mortars, one Blakely gun.

Garrisoned by a detachment of the Palmetto Guard, and by cadets from the Citadel Academy in Charleston. Captain J.P. Thomas, of the Citadel Academy, commanding Blakely gun; Lieutenant C. R. Holmes, of the Citadel Academy, commanding mortars; Lieutenant W.W. Armstrong, of the Citadel Academy, at the mortars; Second Lieutenant Thomas sumter, of the Palmetto Guard, in charge of the forty-two-pounders.

CHANNEL BATTERY. (DID NOT FIRE.)

Captain Calhoun, commanding; First Lieutenant A.M. Wagner; Lieutenant—— Sitgreaves; Second Lieutenant M.C. Preston.

ON JAMES ISLAND.

Major N.G. Evans, A.A.G., commanding.

BATTERY OF TWENTY-FOUR-POUNDERS.

Captain George S. James, commanding.

MORTAR BATTERY.

First Lieutenant W.H. Gibbes, of the Artillery; Lieutenant H.S. Farley; Lieutenant J.E. M'pherson, Washington; Lieutenant T.B. Hayne; Doctor Libby.

UPPER BATTERY. (FIRED 2425 SHOTS.)

Two ten-inch mortars.

LOWER BATTERY.

Two ten-inch mortars.

Captain S.C.Thayer, of the S.C. Navy, commanding.

ON SULLIVAN'S ISLAND.

Brigadier-general John Dunovant, commanding. Lieutenant-colonel Roswell S. Ripley, commanding the Artillery; Captain J. B. Burns, of General Dunovant's staff; Surgeons P.J. Robinson, R.F. Mitchell, and Arthur Lynch; Assistant-surgeons D.W. Taylor, Doctor F.F. Miles, Doctor F.L. Parker.

THE IRON-CLAD FLOATING BATTERY.

(AT THE COVE. FIRED 1900 SHOTS.)

Two forty-two-pounders. Two thirty-two-pounders.

Garrisoned by Company D, of the Artillery. Captain James Hamilton; First Lieutenant J.A.Yates, Second Lieutenant F.H. Harleston.

THE DAHLGREN BATTERY. (NEAR THE FLOATING BATTERY.)

One nine-inch Dahlgren gun.

Garrisoned by Company D, of the Artillery. Captain S.R. Hamilton; Mr. John Wells.

THE ENFILADE BATTERY. (FIRED 1825 SHOTS.)

Garrisoned by Company K, of the Artillery, Captain James H. Hallonquist, Company B, of the Artillery, commanding; First Lieutenant J.Valentine, B.S. Burnett.

MORTAR BATTERY, NO. 1. (BETWEEN FORT MOULTRIE AND THE COVE.)

Captain James H. Hallonquist, Company B, of the Artillery, commanding. Lieutenant O. Blanding, Lieutenant Fleming.

FORT MOULTRIE. (FIRED 1825 SHOTS.)

Three eight-inch columbiads, two thirty-two-pounders, four twenty-four-pounders.

Garrisoned by the Artillery Battalion under Lieutenant-colonel Ripley. Captain W.R. Calhoun, Company A, of the Artillery, executive officer.

SUMTER BATTERY. (FACING SOUTH-SOUTH-WEST.)

Lieutenant Alfred Rhett, Company B, Artillery, commanding; Second Lieutenant John Mitchell, Jun.; Mr. F.D. Blake, Volunteer Engineer.

OBLIQUE BATTERY. (ON THE WEST.)

Two twenty-four-pounders.

Lieutenant C.W. Parker, Company D, of the Artillery.

MORTAR BATTERY, NO. 2. (EAST OF FORT MOULTRIE.)

Two ten-inch mortars.

Captain William Butler, of the Infantry; Lieutenant J.A. Hugenin. E. Mowry, Mr. Blocker, Mr. Billings, and Mr. Rice assisted. This battery was joined to the Maffit Channel Battery.

THE TRAPIER BATTERY. (FIRED 1300 SHOTS.)

Three ten-inch mortars.

Garrisoned by the Marion Artillery, J. Gadsden King, commanding. Lieutenant W.D.H. Kirkwood, J.P. Strohecker, A.M. Huger, E.L. Parker. The Marion Artillery was afterward relieved by the Sumter Guard, under Captain John Russell.

AT MOUNT PLEASANT.

BATTERY. (FIRED 2925 SHOTS.)

Two ten-inch mortars.

Captain Robert Martin of the Infantry, commanding; Lieutenant G.N. Reynolds, Company B, of the Artillery; Lieutenant D.S. Calhoun, of the Infantry.

LEONAUR

ALSO FROM LEONAUR
AVAILABLE IN SOFTCOVER OR HARDCOVER WITH DUST JACKET

AT THEM WITH THE BAYONET *by Donald F. Featherstone*—The first Anglo-Sikh War 1845-1846.

STEPHEN CRANE'S BATTLES *by Stephen Crane*—Nine Decisive Battles Recounted by the Author of 'The Red Badge of Courage'.

THE GURKHA WAR *by H. T. Prinsep*—The Anglo-Nepalese Conflict in North East India 1814-1816.

FIRE & BLOOD *by G. R. Gleig*—The burning of Washington & the battle of New Orleans, 1814, through the eyes of a young British soldier.

SOUND ADVANCE! *by Joseph Anderson*—Experiences of an officer of HM 50th regiment in Australia, Burma & the Gwalior war.

THE CAMPAIGN OF THE INDUS *by Thomas Holdsworth*—Experiences of a British Officer of the 2nd (Queen's Royal) Regiment in the Campaign to Place Shah Shuja on the Throne of Afghanistan 1838 - 1840.

WITH THE MADRAS EUROPEAN REGIMENT IN BURMA *by John Butler*—The Experiences of an Officer of the Honourable East India Company's Army During the First Anglo-Burmese War 1824 - 1826.

IN ZULULAND WITH THE BRITISH ARMY *by Charles L. Norris-Newman*—The Anglo-Zulu war of 1879 through the first-hand experiences of a special correspondent.

BESIEGED IN LUCKNOW *by Martin Richard Gubbins*—The first Anglo-Sikh War 1845-1846.

A TIGER ON HORSEBACK *by L. March Phillips*—The Experiences of a Trooper & Officer of Rimington's Guides - The Tigers - during the Anglo-Boer war 1899 - 1902.

SEPOYS, SIEGE & STORM *by Charles John Griffiths*—The Experiences of a young officer of H.M.'s 61st Regiment at Ferozepore, Delhi ridge and at the fall of Delhi during the Indian mutiny 1857.

CAMPAIGNING IN ZULULAND *by W. E. Montague*—Experiences on campaign during the Zulu war of 1879 with the 94th Regiment.

THE STORY OF THE GUIDES *by G.J. Younghusband*—The Exploits of the Soldiers of the famous Indian Army Regiment from the northwest frontier 1847 - 1900.

LEONAUR

ALSO FROM LEONAUR
AVAILABLE IN SOFTCOVER OR HARDCOVER WITH DUST JACKET

ESCAPE FROM THE FRENCH *by Edward Boys*—A Young Royal Navy Midshipman's Adventures During the Napoleonic War.

THE VOYAGE OF H.M.S. PANDORA *by Edward Edwards R. N. & George Hamilton, edited by Basil Thomson*—In Pursuit of the Mutineers of the Bounty in the South Seas—1790-1791.

MEDUSA *by J. B. Henry Savigny and Alexander Correard and Charlotte-Adélaïde Dard* —Narrative of a Voyage to Senegal in 1816 & The Sufferings of the Picard Family After the Shipwreck of the Medusa.

THE SEA WAR OF 1812 VOLUME 1 *by A. T. Mahan*—A History of the Maritime Conflict.

THE SEA WAR OF 1812 VOLUME 2 *by A. T. Mahan*—A History of the Maritime Conflict.

WETHERELL OF H. M. S. HUSSAR *by John Wetherell*—The Recollections of an Ordinary Seaman of the Royal Navy During the Napoleonic Wars.

THE NAVAL BRIGADE IN NATAL *by C. R. N. Burne*—With the Guns of H. M. S. Terrible & H. M. S. Tartar during the Boer War 1899-1900.

THE VOYAGE OF H. M. S. BOUNTY *by William Bligh*—The True Story of an 18th Century Voyage of Exploration and Mutiny.

SHIPWRECK! *by William Gilly*—The Royal Navy's Disasters at Sea 1793-1849.

KING'S CUTTERS AND SMUGGLERS: 1700-1855 *by E. Keble Chatterton*—A unique period of maritime history-from the beginning of the eighteenth to the middle of the nineteenth century when British seamen risked all to smuggle valuable goods from wool to tea and spirits from and to the Continent.

CONFEDERATE BLOCKADE RUNNER *by John Wilkinson*—The Personal Recollections of an Officer of the Confederate Navy.

NAVAL BATTLES OF THE NAPOLEONIC WARS *by W. H. Fitchett*—Cape St. Vincent, the Nile, Cadiz, Copenhagen, Trafalgar & Others.

PRISONERS OF THE RED DESERT *by R. S. Gwatkin-Williams*—The Adventures of the Crew of the Tara During the First World War.

U-BOAT WAR 1914-1918 *by James B. Connolly/Karl von Schenk*—Two Contrasting Accounts from Both Sides of the Conflict at Sea D uring the Great War.

THE 9TH—THE KING'S (LIVERPOOL REGIMENT) IN THE GREAT WAR 1914 - 1918 *by Enos H. G. Roberts*—Mersey to mud—war and Liverpool men.

THE GAMBARDIER *by Mark Severn*—The experiences of a battery of Heavy artillery on the Western Front during the First World War.

FROM MESSINES TO THIRD YPRES *by Thomas Floyd*—A personal account of the First World War on the Western front by a 2/5th Lancashire Fusilier.

THE IRISH GUARDS IN THE GREAT WAR - VOLUME 1 *by Rudyard Kipling*—Edited and Compiled from Their Diaries and Papers—The First Battalion.

THE IRISH GUARDS IN THE GREAT WAR - VOLUME 1 *by Rudyard Kipling*—Edited and Compiled from Their Diaries and Papers—The Second Battalion.

ARMOURED CARS IN EDEN *by K. Roosevelt*—An American President's son serving in Rolls Royce armoured cars with the British in Mesopatamia & with the American Artillery in France during the First World War.

CHASSEUR OF 1914 *by Marcel Dupont*—Experiences of the twilight of the French Light Cavalry by a young officer during the early battles of the great war in Europe.

TROOP HORSE & TRENCH *by R.A. Lloyd*—The experiences of a British Lifeguardsman of the household cavalry fighting on the western front during the First World War 1914-18.

THE EAST AFRICAN MOUNTED RIFLES *by C.J. Wilson*—Experiences of the campaign in the East African bush during the First World War.

THE LONG PATROL *by George Berrie*—A Novel of Light Horsemen from Gallipoli to the Palestine campaign of the First World War.

THE FIGHTING CAMELIERS *by Frank Reid*—The exploits of the Imperial Camel Corps in the desert and Palestine campaigns of the First World War.

STEEL CHARIOTS IN THE DESERT *by S. C. Rolls*—The first world war experiences of a Rolls Royce armoured car driver with the Duke of Westminster in Libya and in Arabia with T.E. Lawrence.

WITH THE IMPERIAL CAMEL CORPS IN THE GREAT WAR *by Geoffrey Inchbald*—The story of a serving officer with the British 2nd battalion against the Senussi and during the Palestine campaign.